Fc

P

Barbados

GW01091179

Reprinted from *Fodor's Caribbean*

Fodor's Travel Publications, Inc.
New York • Toronto • London •
Sydney • Auckland

ISBN 0–679–02585–5

The legacy of "Little England" reproduced by permission of British Heritage, Box 8200, Harrisburg, PA 17105.

Fodor's Pocket Barbados

Editor: Caroline Haberfeld
Contributors: Bob Blake, Susan Fairbanks, Nigel Fisher, Caroline Liou, Honey Naylor
Creative Director: Fabrizio La Rocca
Cartographer: David Lindroth
Illustrator: Karl Tanner
Cover Photograph: Andre Gallant/Image Bank

Design: Vignelli Associates

Special Sales

MANUFACTURED IN THE UNITED STATES OF AMERICA
10 9 8 7 6 5 4 3 2 1

Contents

Contents

Foreword

Fodor's Pocket Barbados is intended especially for the new or short-term visitor who wants a complete but concise account of the most exciting places to see and the most interesting things to do.

Those who plan to spend more time in the Caribbean, or seek additional information about areas of interest, will want to consult *Fodor's Caribbean* for in-depth coverage of the area.

While every care has been taken to assure the accuracy of the information in this guide, the passage of time will always bring change, and consequently the publisher cannot accept responsibility for errors that may occur.

All prices and opening times quoted here are based on information available to us at press time. Hours and admission fees may change, however, and the prudent traveler will avoid inconvenience by calling ahead.

Fodor's wants to hear about your travel experiences, both pleasant and unpleasant. When a hotel or restaurant fails to live up to its billing, let us know and we will investigate the complaint and revise our entries where the facts warrant it.

Send your letters to the editors of Fodor's Travel Publications, 201 E. 50th St., New York, NY 10022.

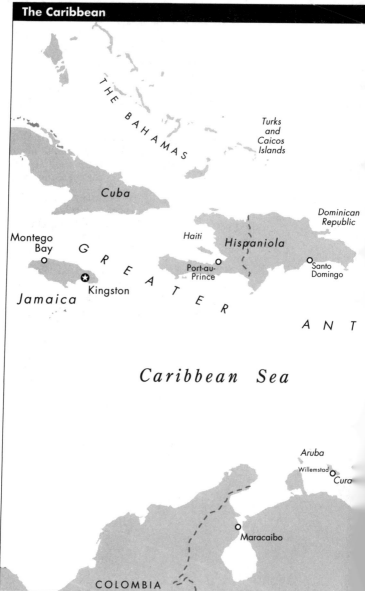

The Caribbean

THE BAHAMAS

Turks
and
Caicos
Islands

Cuba

Dominican
Republic

Montego
Bay

Haiti

Hispaniola

G R E A T E R

Port-au-
Prince

Santo
Domingo

Jamaica

Kingston

A N T

Caribbean Sea

Aruba

Willemstad

Cura

Maracaibo

COLOMBIA

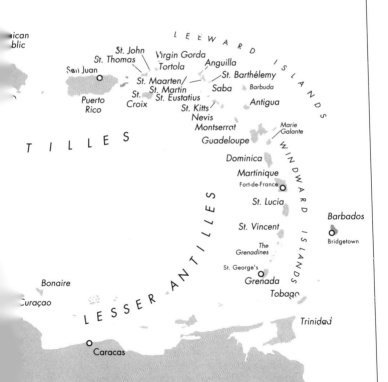

ATLANTIC OCEAN

ican
blic

San Juan

Puerto
Rico

St. Thomas

St. John

Virgin Gorda
Tortola

St. Maarten/
St. Martin
St.   St. Eustatius
Croix   St. Kitts
Nevis
Montserrat

Anguilla

St. Barthélemy

Saba   Barbuda

Antigua

Marie
Galante

Guadeloupe

Dominica

Martinique
Fort-de-France

St. Lucia

St. Vincent

The
Grenadines

St. George's
Grenada

Tobago

Barbados
Bridgetown

L E E W A R D   *I S L A N D S*

W I N D W A R D   *I S L A N D S*

T I L L E S

L E S S E R   A N T I L L E S

Bonaire

Curaçao

Caracas

Trinidad

VENEZUELA

0   200 miles

0   300 km

N

Introduction

Updated by Nigel Fisher

Barbados has a life of its own that goes on after the tourists have packed their sun oils and returned home. Since the government is stable and unemployment is relatively low, the difference between haves and have-nots is less marked—or at least less visible—than on other islands, and visitors are neither fawned upon nor resented for their assumed wealth. Genuinely proud of their country, the quarter million Bajans welcome visitors as privileged guests. Barbados is fine for people who want nothing more than to offer their bodies to the sun; yet the island, unlike many in the Caribbean, is also ideal for travelers who want to discover another life and culture.

Because the beaches of Barbados are open to the public, they lack the privacy that some visitors seek; but the beaches themselves are lovely, and many along the tranquil west coast—in the lee of the northwest trade winds—are backed by first-class resorts. Most of the hotels are situated along the beaches on the southern and southwestern coasts. The British and Canadians often favor the hotels of St. James Parish; Americans (couples more often than singles) tend to prefer the large southcoast resorts.

To the northeast are rolling hills and valleys covered by acres of impenetrable sugarcane. The Atlantic surf pounds the gigantic boulders along the rugged east coast, where the Bajans themselves have their vacation homes. Elsewhere on the island, linked by almost 900 miles of good roads, are historic plantation houses, stalactite-studded caves, a wildlife preserve, and the Andromeda Gardens, one of the most attractive small tropical gardens in the world.

No one is sure whether the name *los Barbados* ("the bearded ones") refers to the beard-like root that hangs from the island's fig trees or to the bearded natives who greeted the Portuguese "discoverer" of the island in 1536. The name Los Barbados was still current almost a century later when the British landed—by accident—in what is now Holetown in St. James Parish. They colonized the island in 1627 and remained until it achieved independence in 1966.

Barbadians retain a British accent. Afternoon tea is habitual at numerous hotels. Cricket is still the national sport, producing some of the world's top cricket players. Polo is played in winter. The British tradition of dressing for dinner is firmly entrenched; a few luxury hotels require tie and jacket at dinner, and in good restaurants most women will consider themselves inappropriately dressed in anything less formal than a sundress. (A daytime stroll in a swimsuit is as inappropriate in Bridgetown as it would be on New York's 5th Avenue.) Yet the island's atmosphere is hardly stuffy. When the boat you ordered for noon doesn't arrive until 12:30, you can expect a cheerful response, "He okay, mon, he just on Caribbean time." Translation: No one, including you, needs to be in a hurry here.

1 Essential Information

Before You Go

Tourist Information

Each island has a U.S.–based tourist board; they're good sources of general information, up-to-date calendars of events, and listings of hotels, restaurants, sights, and shops. The **Caribbean Tourism Organization** (20 E. 46th St., New York, NY 10017–2452, tel. 212/682–0435) is another resource, especially for information on the islands that don't have tourist offices in the United States.

Contact the **Barbados Board of Tourism,** 800 2nd Ave., New York, NY 10017, tel. 212/986–6516; or 3440 Wilshire Blvd., Suite 1215, Los Angeles, CA 90010, tel. 213/380–2199. In Canada: 5160 Yonge St., Suite 1800, N. York, Ont. M2N–6L9, tel. 416/512–6569; 615 Dorchester, Montreal, Suite 960, Montreal, P.Q. H3B 1P5, tel. 514/861–0085. In the United Kingdom: 263 Tottenham Court Rd., London W1P 9AA, tel. 441/636–9448.

The Department of State's **Citizens Emergency Center** issues Consular Information Sheets, which cover crime, security, and health risks as well as embassy locations, entry requirements, currency regulations, and other routine matters. (Travel warnings, which counsel travelers to avoid a country entirely, are issued in extreme cases.) For the latest travel advisories, stop in at any passport office, consulate, or embassy; call the interactive hot line (tel. 202/647–5225); or, with your PC's modem, tap into the Bureau of Consular Affairs's computer bulletin board (tel. 202/647–9225).

Festivals and Seasonal Events

February The Holetown Festival commemorates the island's first settlement in 1627 with a week of fairs, street markets, and revelry. Fifteenth- and 16th-century religious chorales echo in village churches, while an unmistakably modern beat animates the fairgrounds.

April The two-day Oistins Fish Festival, held every Easter, commemorates the signing of the Charter of Barbados and honors the local fishing industry: Fishing competitions, boat races, street entertainment, and open-air bazaars abound. Steel bands and food stalls make the events all the more lively, and spectators mingle Bajan crowds on the beaches, in the marketplace, and in quaint roadside rum shops.

May The three-day Barbados Caribbean Jazz Festival is held at the end of the month. Performances of original compositions and traditional jazz take place in several locations in Bridgetown.

July Cutting across July and August, the Crop-Over Festival cheers for the end of the sugarcane harvest. Tents ring with the fierce battle of Calypsonians for the coveted Calypso Monarch award, and the air is redolent with smells of Bajan cooking as part of the "Bridgetown Market" street fair. The "Cohobblopot" blends drama, dance, and music with the crowning of the king and queen of costume bands, and both the King of Calypso and the Clown Prince are crowned on the night of "Pic-O-de-Crop Show." The festival closes with "Kadooment Day"—a national holiday—but not before fireworks fill the sky and costumed bands fill the streets with pulsating Caribbean rhythms.

November Through Independence Day, November 30, residents show off their music, singing, dancing, acting, and writing talents during National Independence Festival of the Creative Arts.

December The first weekend of December marks the annual Run Barbados International Road Race Series. Both a marathon over paved roads along the shore and a 10k race in and around Bridgetown attract competitors from around the world. Among the top prizes for overseas entrants are airfare and hotel accommodations for the next year's race!

What to Pack

Pack light because baggage carts are scarce at the airport and luggage restrictions are tight.

Clothing Dress in Barbados is light and casual. Bring loose-fitting clothes made of natural fabrics to see you through days of heat and high humidity. Take a coverup for the beaches, not only to protect you from the sun, but also to wear to and from your hotel room. Bathing suits and immodest attire are frowned upon off the beach. A sun hat is advisable, but you don't have to pack one, since inexpensive straw hats are available everywhere. For shopping and sightseeing, bring walking shorts, jeans, T-shirts, longsleeve cotton shirts, slacks, and sundresses. You'll need a sweater in the many glacially airconditioned hotels and restaurants, for protection from the trade winds, and at higher altitudes. Evenings are fairly casual; women usually wear sundresses and some luxury resorts request jacket and tie for men.

Adapters, Converters, Transformers

The general rule in Barbados is 110 and 120 volts AC, and the outlets take the same two-prong plugs found in the United States, but there are a number of exceptions. To be sure, check with your hotel when making reservations.

You may need an adapter plug, plus a converter, which reduces the voltage entering the appliance from 220 to 110 volts. There are converters for high-wattage appliances (such as hair dryers), low-wattage items (such as electric toothbrushes and razors), and combination models. Hotels sometimes have outlets marked "For Shavers Only" near the sink; these are 110-volt outlets for low-wattage appliances; don't use them for a high-wattage appliance. If you're traveling with a laptop computer, especially an older one, you may need a transformer—a type of converter used with electronic-circuitry products. Newer laptop computers are autosensing, operating equally well on 110 and 220 volts (so you need only the appropriate adapter plug). When in doubt, consult your appliance's owner's manual or the manufacturer. Or get a copy of the free brochure "Foreign Electricity is No Deep Dark Secret," published by adapterconverter manufacturer Franzus (Murtha Industrial Park, Box 142, Beacon Falls, CT 06403, tel. 203/723–6664; send a stamped, self-addressed envelope when ordering).

Miscellaneous

Bring a spare pair of eyeglasses and sunglasses, and if you have a health problem that may require you to purchase a prescription drug, have your doctor write a prescription using its generic name, since nomenclature varies from island to island. Better still, take enough to last the duration of the trip: Although you can probably find what you need in the pharmacies, you may need a local doctor's prescription. You'll want an umbrella during the rainy season; leave the plastic or nylon raincoats at home, since they're extremely uncomfortable in hot, humid weather. Bring suntan lotion and film from home; they're much more expensive on the islands. You'll need insect repellent, too, especially if you plan to walk through rain forests or visit during the rainy season. Don't forget to pack a list of the addresses of offices that supply refunds for lost or stolen traveler's checks.

Luggage Free baggage allowances on an airline depend
Regulations on the airline, the route, and the class of your ticket. In general, on domestic flights and on international flights between the United States and foreign destinations, you are entitled to check two bags—neither exceeding 62 inches, or 158 centimeters (length + width + height), or weighing more than 70 pounds (32 kilograms). A third piece may be brought aboard as a carryon; its total dimensions are generally limited to less than 45 inches (114 centimeters), so it will fit easily under the seat in front of you or in the overhead compartment. There are variations, so ask in advance. The only rule, a Federal Aviation Administration safety regulation that pertains to carry-on baggage on U.S. airlines, requires only that carryons be properly stowed and allows the airline to limit allowances and tailor them to different aircraft and operational conditions. Charges for excess, oversize, or overweight pieces vary, so inquire before you pack.

If you are flying between two foreign destinations, note that baggage allowances may be determined not by the piece method but by the weight method, which generally allows 88 pounds (40 kilograms) of luggage in first class, 66 pounds (30 kilograms) in business class, and 44 pounds (20 kilograms) in economy. If your flight between two cities abroad *connects* with your transatlantic or transpacific flight, the piece method still applies.

Safeguarding Your Luggage Before leaving home, itemize your bags' contents and their worth; this list will help you estimate the extent of your loss if your bags go astray. To minimize that risk, tag them inside and out with your name, address, and phone number. (If you use your home address, cover it so that potential thieves can't see it.) At check-in, make sure that the tag attached by baggage handlers bears the correct three-letter code for your destination. If your bags do not arrive with you, or if you detect damage, do not leave the airport until you've filed a written report with the airline.

Getting Money from Home

Cash Machines Automated-teller machines (ATMs) are proliferating; many are tied to international networks such as **Cirrus** and **Plus**, both of which have expanded their service in the Caribbean. You can use your bank card at ATMs away from home to withdraw money from your checking account and get cash advances on a credit-card account (providing your card has been programmed with a personal identification number, or PIN). Check in advance on limits on withdrawals and cash advances within specified periods. Ask whether your bank-card or credit-card PIN number will need to be reprogrammed for use in the area you'll be visiting—a possibility if the number has more than four digits. Remember that on cash advances you are charged interest from the day you get the money from ATMs as well as from tellers. And note that, although transaction fees for ATM withdrawals abroad will probably be higher than fees for withdrawals at home, Cirrus and Plus exchange rates tend to be good. Be sure to plan ahead: Obtain ATM locations and the names of affiliated cash-machine networks before departure. For specific foreign Cirrus locations, call 800/4–CIRRUS; for foreign Plus locations, consult the Plus directory at your local bank.

American Express Cardholder Services The company's **Express Cash** system lets you withdraw cash and/or traveler's checks from a worldwide network of 57,000 American Express dispensers and participating bank ATMs. You must *enroll first* (call 800/CASH–NOW for a form and allow two weeks for processing). Withdrawals are charged not to your card but to a designated bank account. You can withdraw up to $1,000 per seven-day period on the basic card, more if your card is gold or platinum. There is a 2% fee (minimum $2.50, maximum $10) for each cash transaction, and a 1% fee for traveler's checks (except for the platinum card), which are available only from American Express dispensers.

At AmEx offices, cardholders can also cash personal checks for up to $1,000 in any seven-day period in U.S. territory (21 days abroad); of this, $200 can be in cash, more if available, with the balance paid in traveler's checks, for which all but platinum cardholders pay a 1% fee. Higher limits apply to the gold and platinum cards.

Wiring Money You don't have to be a cardholder to send or receive an **American Express MoneyGram** for up to $10,000. To send one, go to an American Express MoneyGram agent, pay up to $1,000 with a credit card and anything over that in cash, and phone a transaction reference number to your intended recipient, who needs only present identification and the reference number to the nearest MoneyGram agent to pick up the cash. There are MoneyGram agents in more than 60 countries (call 800/543–4080 for locations). Fees range from 5% to 10%, depending on the amount and how you pay. You can't use American Express, which is really a convenience card—only Discover, MasterCard, and Visa credit cards.

You can also use **Western Union.** To wire money, take either cash or a check to the nearest office. (Or you can order money sent by phone, using a credit card.) Money sent from the United States or Canada will be available for pickup at agent locations in the Caribbean within minutes, and fees are roughly 5%–10%. (Note that once the money is in the system it can be picked up at *any* location. You don't have to miss your train waiting for it to arrive in City A, because if there's an agent in City B, where you're headed, you can pick it up there, too.) There are approximately 20,000 agents worldwide (call 800/325–6000 for locations).

Traveling with Cameras, Camcorders, and Laptops

About Film and Cameras If your camera is new or if you haven't used it for a while, shoot and develop a few rolls of film before leaving home. Pack some lens tissue and an extra battery for your built-in light meter, and invest in an inexpensive skylight filter, to both protect your lens and provide some definition in hazy shots. Store film in a cool, dry place—never in the car's glove compartment or on the shelf under the rear window.

Films above ISO 400 are more sensitive to damage from airport security X rays than others; very high-speed films, ISO 1000 and above, are exceedingly vulnerable. To protect your film, don't put it in checked luggage; carry it with you in a plastic bag and ask for a hand inspection. Such requests are honored at U.S. airports, but may not be by the inspector abroad. Don't depend on a lead-lined bag to protect film in checked luggage—the airline may very well turn up the dosage of radiation to see what you've got in there. Airport metal detectors do not harm film, although you'll set off the alarm if you walk through one with a roll in your pocket. Call the Kodak Information Center (tel. 800/242–2424) for details.

About Camcorders Before your trip, put new or long-unused camcorders through their paces, and practice panning and zooming. Invest in a skylight filter to protect the lens, and check the lithium battery that lights up the LCD (liquid crystal display) modes. As for the rechargeable nickel-cadmium batteries that are the camera's power source, take along an extra pair, so while you're using your camcorder you'll have one battery ready and another recharging. Most newer camcorders are equipped with the battery (which generally slides or clicks onto the camera body) and, to recharge it, with what's known as a universal or worldwide AC adapter charger (or multivoltage converter) that can be used whether the voltage is 110 or 220. All that's needed is the appropriate plug.

About Videotape Unlike still-camera film, videotape is not damaged by X rays. However, it may well be harmed by the magnetic field of a walk-through metal detector. Airport security personnel may want you to turn the camcorder on to prove that that's what it is, so make sure the battery is charged when you get to the airport. Note that most Caribbean islands operate on the National Television System Committee video standard (NTSC), like the United States and Canada. Blank tapes bought in the Caribbean can be used for NTSC camcorder taping, however—although you'll probably find they cost more in the islands and wish you'd brought an adequate supply along.

Staying Healthy

Few real hazards threaten the health of a visitor to Barbados. The small lizards that seem to have overrun the island are harmless, and poisonous snakes are hard to find. The worst problem may well be a tiny sand fly known as the "no see'um," which tends to appear after a rain, near wet or swampy ground, and around sunset. If you feel particularly vulnerable to insect bites, bring along a good repellent.

The worst problem tends to be sunburn or sunstroke. Even people who are not normally bothered by strong sun should head into this area with a long-sleeve shirt, a hat, and long pants or a beach wrap. These are essential for a day on a boat but are also advisable for midday at the beach and whenever you go out sightseeing. Also carry some sun-block lotion for nose, ears, and other sensitive areas such as eyelids, ankles, etc. Limit your sun time for the first few days until you become used to the heat. And be sure to drink enough liquids.

No special shots are required for Barbados.

Scuba divers take note: PADI recommends that you not scuba dive and fly within a 24-hour period.

Finding a Doctor The **International Association for Medical Assistance to Travelers** (IAMAT, 417 Center St., Lewiston, NY 14092, tel. 716/754–4883; 40 Regal Rd., Guelph, Ont. N1K 1B5; 57 Voirets, 1212 Grand-Lancy, Geneva, Switzerland) publishes a worldwide directory of English-speaking physicians whose qualifications meet IAMAT standards and who have agreed to treat members for a set fee. Membership is free.

Insurance

Most tour operators, travel agents, and insurance agents sell specialized health-and-accident, flight, trip-cancellation, and luggage insurance as well as comprehensive policies with some or all of these features. But before you make any purchase, review your existing health and homeowner policies to find out whether they cover expenses incurred while traveling.

Health-and-Accident Insurance Supplemental health-and-accident insurance for travelers is usually a part of comprehensive policies. Specific policy provisions vary, but they tend to address three general areas, beginning with reimbursement for medical expenses caused by illness or an accident during a trip. Such policies may reimburse anywhere from $1,000 to $150,000 worth of medical expenses; dental benefits may also be included. A second common feature is the personal-accident, or death-and-dismemberment, provision, which pays a lump sum to your beneficiaries if you die or to you if you lose one or both limbs or your eyesight. This is similar to the flight insurance described below, although it is not necessarily limited to accidents involving airplanes or even other "common carriers" (buses, trains, and ships) and can be in effect 24 hours a day. The lump sum awarded can range from $15,000 to $500,000. A third area generally addressed by these policies is medical assistance (referrals, evacuation, or repatriation and other services). Some policies reimburse travelers for the cost of such services; others may automatically enroll you as a member of a particular medical-assistance company.

Flight Insurance This insurance, often bought as a last-minute impulse at the airport, pays a lump sum to a beneficiary when a plane crashes and the insured dies (and sometimes to a surviving passenger who loses eyesight or a limb); thus it supplements the airlines' own coverage as described in the limits-of-liability paragraphs on your ticket (up to $75,000 on international flights, $20,000 on domestic ones—and that is generally subject to litigation). Charging an airline ticket to a major credit card often automatically signs you up for flight insurance; in this case, the coverage may also embrace travel by bus, train, and ship.

Baggage Insurance In the event of loss, damage, or theft on international flights, airlines limit their liability to $20 per kilogram for checked baggage (roughly about $640 per 70-pound bag) and $400 per passenger for unchecked baggage. On domestic flights, the ceiling is $1,250 per passenger. Excess-valuation insurance can be bought directly from the airline at check-in but leaves your bags vulnerable on the ground.

Trip Insurance There are two sides to this coin. **Trip-cancellation-and-interruption insurance** protects you in the event you are unable to undertake or finish your trip. **Default or bankruptcy insurance** protects you against a supplier's failure to deliver. Consider the former if your airline ticket, cruise, or package tour does not allow changes or cancellations. The amount of coverage to buy should equal the cost of your trip should you, a traveling companion, or a family member get sick, forcing you to stay home, plus the non-discounted one-way airline ticket you would need to buy if you had to return home early. Read the fine print carefully; pay attention to sections defining "family member" and "preexisting medical conditions." A characteristic quirk of default policies is that they often do not cover default by travel agencies or default by a tour operator, airline, or cruise line if you bought your tour and the coverage directly from the firm in question. To reduce your need for default insurance, give preference to tours packaged by members of the United States Tour Operators Association (USTOA), which maintains a fund to reimburse clients in the event of member defaults. Even better, pay for travel arrangements with a major credit card, so you can refuse to pay the bill if services have not been rendered—and let the card company fight your battles.

Comprehensive Policies Companies supplying comprehensive policies with some or all of the above features include **Access America, Inc.,** underwritten by BCS Insurance Company (Box 11188, Richmond, VA 23230, tel. 800/284–8300); **Carefree Travel Insurance,** underwritten by The Hartford (Box 310, 120 Mineola Blvd., Mineola, NY 11501, tel. 516/294–0220 or 800/323–3149); **Tele-Trip** (Mutual of Omaha Plaza, Box 31762, Omaha, NE 68131, tel. 800/228–9792), a subsidiary of Mutual of Omaha; **The Travelers Companies** (1 Tower Sq., Hartford, CT 06183, tel. 203/277–0111 or 800/243–3174); **Travel Guard International,** underwritten by Transamerica Occidental Life Companies (1145 Clark St., Stevens Point, WI 54481, tel. 715/345–0505 or 800/782–5151); and **Wallach and Company, Inc.** (107 W. Federal St., Box 480, Middleburg, VA 22117, tel. 703/687–3166 or 800/237–6615), underwritten by Lloyds, London. These companies may also offer the above types of insurance separately.

Student and Youth Travel

Barbados is not as far out of a student's budget as you might expect. There are fine camping facilities as well as inexpensive guest houses and small no-frills hotels.

Travel Agencies The foremost U.S. student travel agency is **Council Travel,** a subsidiary of the nonprofit Council on International Educational Exchange. It specializes in low-cost travel arrangements, is the exclusive U.S. agent for several discount cards, and, with its sister CIEE subsidiary, **Council Charter,** is a source of airfare bargains. The Council Charter brochure and CIEE's twice-yearly *Student Travels* magazine, which details its programs, are available at the Council Travel office at CIEE headquarters (205 E. 42nd Street, New York, NY 10017, tel. 212/661–1450) and at 37 branches in college towns nationwide (free in person, $1 by mail). The **Educational Travel Center** (ETC, 438 N. Francis St., Madison, WI 53703, tel. 608/256–5551) also offers low-cost rail passes, domestic and international airline tickets (mostly for flights departing from Chicago), and other budgetwise travel arrangements. Other travel agencies catering to students include **Travel Management International** (TMI, 18 Prescott St., Suite 4, Cambridge, MA 02138, tel. 617/

661–8187) and **Travel Cuts** (187 College St., Toronto, Ont. M5T 1P7, tel. 416/979–2406).

Traveling with Children

Barbados and its resorts are increasingly sensitive to the needs of families. Children's programs are part of all major new developments. Baby food is easy to find, but outside major hotels you may not find such items as high chairs and cribs. English is widely spoken, so there is no language barrier.

Getting There All children, including infants, must have a passport for foreign travel.

Airfares What you will pay for your children's tickets depends on your starting and ending points. In some cases, the fare for infants under 2 not occupying a seat is 10% of the accompanying adult's fare, and children ages 2–11 pay half to two-thirds of the adult fare. In other instances, children under 2 not occupying a seat travel free, and older children currently travel on the "lowest applicable" adult fare, as on flights within the United States. Other routes have still other rules, so check ahead.

Safety Seats The FAA recommends the use of safety seats aloft and details approved models in the free leaflet **"Child/Infant Safety Seats Recommended for Use in Aircraft"** (available from the Federal Aviation Administration, APA–200, 800 Independence Ave. SW, Washington, DC 20591, tel. 202/267–3479). Airline policy varies. U.S. carriers must allow FAA-approved models, but because these seats are strapped into a regular passenger seat, they may require that parents buy a ticket even for an infant under 2 who would otherwise ride free. Foreign carriers may not allow infant seats, may charge the child's rather than the infant's fare for their use, or may require you to hold your baby during takeoff and landing, thus defeating the seat's purpose.

Facilities Aloft Airlines do provide other facilities and services for children, such as children's meals and free-standing bassinets (to those sitting in seats on the bulkhead, where there's enough legroom to accommodate them). Make your request when reserving. The annual February/March issue of

Family Travel Times gives details of the children's services of dozens of airlines (*see below*). "Kids and Teens in Flight" (free from the U.S. Department of Transportation, tel. 202/366–2220) offers tips for children flying alone.

Tour **GrandTravel** (6900 Wisconsin Ave., Suite 706,
Operators Chevy Chase, MD 20815, tel. 301/986–0790 or 800/247–7651) offers international and domestic tours for grandparents traveling with their grandchildren. The catalogue, as charmingly written and illustrated as a children's book, positively invites armchair traveling with lapsitters aboard. **Rascals in Paradise** (650 5th St., Suite 505, San Francisco, CA 94107, tel. 415/978–9800 or 800/872–7225) specializes in programs for families.

Villa Rentals Villa rentals are abundant, often economical, and great for families; island tourist boards can usually refer you to the appropriate realtors. When you book these, be sure to ask about the availability of baby-sitters, housekeepers, and medical facilities.

Publications **Family Travel Times,** published 10 times a year
Newsletter by Travel With Your Children (TWYCH, 45 W. 18th St., 7th Floor Tower, New York, NY 10011, tel. 212/206–0688; annual subscription $55), covers destinations, types of vacations, and modes of travel; an airline issue comes out every other year (the last one, February/March 1993, is sold to nonsubscribers for $10). On Wednesday, the staff answers subscribers' questions on specific destinations.

Books *Great Vacations with Your Kids,* by Dorothy Jordan and Marjorie Cohen ($13; Penguin USA, 120 Woodbine St., Bergenfield, NJ 07621, tel. 800/253–6476) and *Traveling with Children—And Enjoying It,* by Arlene K. Butler ($11.95 plus $3 shipping per book; Globe Pequot Press, Box 833, Old Saybrook, CT 06475, tel. 800/243–0495 or 800/962–0973 in CT) both help you plan your trip with children, from toddlers to teens. Also from Globe Pequot is *Recommended Family Resorts in the United States, Canada, and the Caribbean,* by Jane Wilford with Janet Tice ($12.95), which describes 100 resorts at length and includes a "Children's World" section describing activities and facilities as part of each entry.

Hints for Travelers with Disabilities

The Caribbean has not progressed as far as other areas of the world in terms of accommodating travelers with disabilities, and very few attractions and sights are equipped with ramps, elevators, or wheelchair-accessible rest rooms. However, major new properties are beginning to do their planning with the needs of travelers with mobility problems and hearing and visual impairments in mind. Wherever possible in our lodging listings, we indicate if special facilities are available.

Accommodations   A number of cruise ships, such as the *QE II* and the Norwegian Cruise Line's *Seaward*, have recently adapted some of their cabins to meet the needs of passengers with disabilities. To make sure that a given establishment provides adequate access, ask about specific facilities when making a reservation or consider booking through a travel agent who specializes in travel for the disabled (*see below*).

Travel   **Tomorrow's Level of Care** (TLC, Box 470299,
Agencies and   Brooklyn, NY 11247, tel. 718/756–0794 or 800/
Tour   932–2012) was started by two Barbadian nurses
Operators   who develop unique vacation programs tailored to travelers with mobility problems and their families. They can arrange everything from accommodations to entire packages. **Directions Unlimited** (720 N. Bedford Rd., Bedford Hills, NY 10507, tel. 914/241–1700), a travel agency, has expertise in tours and cruises for the disabled; **Evergreen Travel Service** (4114 198th St. SW, Suite 13, Lynnwood, WA 98036, tel. 206/776–1184 or 800/435–2288) operates Wings on Wheels Tours for those in wheelchairs, White Cane Tours for the blind, and tours for the deaf and makes group and independent arrangements for travelers with any disability. **Flying Wheels Travel** (143 W. Bridge St., Box 382, Owatonna, MN 55060, tel. 800/535–6790 or 800/722–9351 in MN), a tour operator and travel agency, arranges international tours, cruises, and independent travel itineraries for people with mobility disabilities. **Nautilus,** at the same

address as TIDE (*see below*), packages tours for the disabled internationally.

Information Sources Several organizations provide travel information for people with disabilities, usually for a membership fee, and some publish newsletters and bulletins. Among them are the **Information Center for Individuals with Disabilities** (Fort Point Pl., 27–43 Wormwood St., Boston, MA 02210, tel. 617/727–5540 or 800/462–5015 in MA between 11 and 4, or leave message; TDD/TTY tel. 617/345–9743); **Mobility International USA** (Box 3551, Eugene, OR 97403, voice and TDD tel. 503/343–1284), the U.S. branch of an international organization based in Britain and present in 39 countries; **MossRehab Hospital Travel Information Service** (1200 W. Tabor Rd., Philadelphia, PA 19141, tel. 215/456–9603, TDD tel. 215/456–9602); The **Society for the Advancement of Travel for the Handicapped** (SATH, 347 5th Ave., Suite 610, New York, NY 10016, tel. 212/447–7284, fax 212/725–8253); the **Travel Industry and Disabled Exchange** (TIDE, 5435 Donna Ave., Tarzana, CA 91356, tel. 818/368–5648); and **Travelin' Talk** (Box 3534, Clarksville, TN 37043, tel. 615/552–6670).

Publications In addition to the fact sheets, newsletters, and books mentioned above are several free publications available from the Consumer Information Center (Pueblo, CO 81009): "New Horizons for the Air Traveler with a Disability," a U.S. Department of Transportation booklet describing changes resulting from the 1986 Air Carrier Access Act and those still to come from the 1990 Americans with Disabilities Act (include Department 608Y in the address), and the Airport Operators Council's *Access Travel: Airports* (Dept. 5804), which describes facilities and services for the disabled at more than 500 airports worldwide.

Twin Peaks Press (Box 129, Vancouver, WA 98666, tel. 206/694–2462 or 800/637–2256) publishes the *Directory of Travel Agencies for the Disabled* ($19.95), listing more than 370 agencies worldwide; *Travel for the Disabled* ($19.95), listing some 500 access guides and accessible places worldwide; the *Directory of Accessible Van Rentals* ($9.95) for campers and RV travelers worldwide; and *Wheelchair Vagabond* ($14.95), a collection of personal travel tips. Add $2 per book for shipping.

Hints for Older Travelers

Special facilities, rates, and package deals for older travelers are rare. When planning your trip, be sure to inquire about everything from senior-citizen discounts to available medical facilities. Focus on your vacation needs: Are you interested in sightseeing, activities, golf, ecotourism, the beach? Accessibility is an important consideration. When booking, inquire whether you can easily get to the things that you enjoy.

Organizations The **American Association of Retired Persons** (AARP, 601 E. St. NW, Washington, DC 20049, tel. 202/434–2277) provides independent travelers with the Purchase Privilege Program, which offers discounts on hotels, car rentals, and sightseeing. AARP also arranges group tours, cruises, and apartment living through AARP Travel Experience from American Express (400 Pinnacle Way, Suite 450, Norcross, GA 30071, tel. 800/927–0111); these can be booked through travel agents, except for the cruises, which must be booked directly (tel. 800/745–4567). AARP membership is open to those 50 and over; annual dues are $8 per person or couple.

Two other membership organizations offer discounts on lodgings, car rentals, and other travel products, along with such nontravel perks as magazines and newsletters. The **National Council of Senior Citizens** (1331 F St. NW, Washington, DC 20004, tel. 202/347–8800) is a nonprofit advocacy group with some 5,000 local clubs across the United States; membership costs $12 per person or couple annually. **Mature Outlook** (6001 N. Clark St., Chicago, IL 60660, tel. 800/336–6330), a Sears Roebuck & Co. subsidiary with 800,000 members, charges $9.95 for an annual membership.

Note: When using any senior-citizen identification card for reduced hotel rates, mention it when booking, not when checking out. At restaurants, show your card before you're seated;

discounts may be limited to certain menus, days, or hours. If you are renting a car, ask about promotional rates that might improve on your senior-citizen discount.

Educational Travel **Elderhostel** (75 Federal St., 3rd floor, Boston, MA 02110, tel. 617/426–7788) is a nonprofit organization that has had inexpensive study programs for people 60 and older since 1975. Programs take place at more than 1,800 educational institutions in the United States, Canada, and 45 countries overseas, and courses cover everything from marine science to Greek myths and cowboy poetry. Participants generally attend lectures in the morning and spend the afternoon sightseeing or on field trips; they live in dorms on the host campuses. Unique home-stay programs are offered in a few countries. Fees for the two- to three-week international trips—including room, board, tuition, and transportation from the United States—range from $1,800 to $4,500.

Tour Operators **Saga International Holidays** (222 Berkeley St., Boston, MA 02116, tel. 800/343–0273), which specializes in group travel for people over 60, offers a selection of variously priced tours and cruises covering five continents. If you want to take your grandchildren, look into GrandTravel (*see* Traveling with Children, *above*).

Publications *The International Health Guide for Senior Citizen Travelers,* by W. Robert Lange, MD ($4.95 plus $1.50 for shipping; Pilot Books, 103 Cooper St., Babylon, NY 11702, tel. 516/422–2225), advises on pretrip planning and on traveling with specific medical conditions. It includes a list of what to pack in a basic medical travel kit and a chart showing how to adjust insulin dosages when flying across multiple time zones. *Get Up and Go* ($10.95 plus $1.75 postage, Gem Publishing Group, Box 50820, Reno, NV 89513, tel. 702/786–7419) is a 325-page handbook of travel tips and deals for Americans over 49; the same organization publishes the monthly *Mature Traveler* newsletter ($24.50 annually), covering senior travel bargains and programs.

Arriving and Departing

By Plane

Grantley Adams Airport in Barbados is a Caribbean hub. There are daily flights from New York (via San Juan); however, **American Airlines** (tel. 800/433–7300) and **BWIA** (tel. 800/JET-BWIA) both have nonstop flights from New York. There are direct flights from Miami on BWIA. From Canada, **Air Canada** (tel. 800/776–3000) connects from Montreal through New York or Miami and flies nonstop from Toronto. From London, **British Airways** (tel. 800/247–9297) has nonstop service and BWIA connects through Trinidad.

Flights to St. Vincent, St. Lucia, Trinidad, and other islands are scheduled on **LIAT** (tel. 809/462–0801) and BWIA; Air St. Vincent/Air Mustique links Barbados with St. Vincent and the Grenadines.

From the Airport Airport taxis are not metered. A large sign at the airport announces the fixed rate to each hotel or area, stated in both Barbados and U.S. dollars (about $20 to the west coast hotels, $13 to the south coast ones). The new highway around Bridgetown saves time and trouble in getting up the western coast.

By Boat

A popular cruise port, Barbados has room for eight ships (which is some indication of how crowded the Bridgetown shops can be). Bridgetown Harbour is located on the northwest side of Carlisle Bay, and most cruise ships organize transportation to and from the **Carlisle Bay Centre,** a "hotel without rooms" for passengers on shore excursions. The CBC provides changing facilities, a restaurant, gift shops, and watersports facilities—including floats, snorkel equipment, Sunfish sailboats, waterskiing, Windsurfers—for a nominal fee.

Passports and Visas

U.S. and Canadian citizens need proof of citizenship plus a return or ongoing ticket to enter the country. Acceptable proof of citizenship is a valid passport or an original birth certificate and a photo ID; a voter registration card is not acceptable. British citizens need a valid passport.

Customs and Duties

Barbados is a noted free port where most duty-free items can be bought over the counter when you show your passport or air/sea ticket. Items that must be delivered to your point of departure are tobacco, wines, and video/stereo/computer equipment.

Language

English is spoken everywhere, sometimes accented with the phrases and lilt of a Bajan dialect.

Precautions

Beach vendors of coral jewelry and beachwear will not hesitate to offer you their wares. The degree of persistence varies, and some of their jewelry offerings are good; sharp bargaining is expected on both sides. One hotel's brochure gives sound advice: "Please realize that encouraging the beach musicians means you may find yourself listening to the same three tunes over and over for the duration of your stay."

Water The water on the island, both in hotels and in restaurants, has been treated and is safe to drink.

Insects Insects aren't much of a problem on Barbados, but if you plan to hike or spend time on secluded beaches, it's wise to use insect repellent.

Toxic Tree Little green apples that fall from the large branches of the manchineel tree may look tempting, but they are poisonous to eat and toxic to the touch. Even taking shelter under the tree when it rains can give you blisters. Most manchineels are identified with signs; if you do come in contact with one, go to the nearest hotel and have someone there phone for a physician.

Crime Don't invite trouble by leaving valuables unattended on the beach or in plain sight in your room, and don't pick up hitchhikers.

Staying in Barbados

Important Addresses

Tourist Information: **The Barbados Board of Tourism** is on Harbour Road in Bridgetown (tel. 809/427–2623). Hours are 8:30–4:30 Monday–Friday. There are also information booths, staffed by Board representatives at Grantley Adams International Airport and at Bridgetown's Deep Water Harbour.

Emergencies **Emergency:** tel. 119.
Ambulance: tel. 809/426–1113.
Police: tel. 112.
Fire department: tel. 113.
Scuba diving accidents: Divers' Alert Network (DAN) (tel. 919/684–8762 or 919/684–2948). Barbados decompression chamber, Barbados Defense Force, St. Ann's Fort, Garrison, St. Michael Parish (tel. 809/427–8819).

Currency

One Barbados dollar (BDS$1) equals about U.S.50¢. Because the value of the Barbados dollar is pegged to that of the U.S. dollar, the ratio remains constant. Both currencies and the Canadian dollar are accepted everywhere on the island, but changing your money to Barbados dollars will get you slightly better value. Prices quoted throughout this chapter are in U.S. dollars unless noted otherwise.

Taxes and Service Charges

At the airport you must pay a departure tax of BDS$25 (about U.S.$12) in either currency before leaving Barbados.

A 10% service charge is added to your hotel bill and to most restaurant checks; any additional tip recognizes extraordinary service. When no service charge is added, tip maids $1 per room per day, waiters 10% to 15%, taxi drivers 10%. Airport porters and bellboys expect BDS$2 (U.S.$1) per bag.

Guided Tours

For an island of its size (14 miles by 21 miles), Barbados has a lot to see. A bus or taxi tour, which can be arranged by your hotel, is a good way to get your bearings. **L. E. Williams Tour Co.** (tel. 809/427–1043) offers an 80-mile island tour for about $50; a bus picks you up between 8:30 and 9:30 AM and takes you through Bridgetown, the St. James beach area, past the Animal Flower Cave, Farley Hill, Cherry Tree Hill, Morgan Lewis Mill, the east coast, St. John's Church, Sam Lord's Castle, Oistin's fishing village, and to St. Michael Parish, with drinks along the way and a West Indian lunch at the Atlantis Hotel in Bathsheba.

Sally Shern operates **VIP Tours** (Hillcrest Villa, Upton, St. Michael Parish, tel. 809/429–4617), custom-tailored to each client, whom she picks up in an air-conditioned Mercedes-Benz. Bajan-born Ms. Shern knows her island well and provides the unusual and unique: a champagne lunch at Sunbury Plantation House, a swim at her favorite beach. **Bajan Helicopters** offers an eagle's-eye view of Barbados (The Wharf, Bridgetown, tel. 809/431–0069). Depending upon the time spent aloft, prices per person range from U.S.$60 for 20 minutes to U.S.$90 for 30 minutes.

Custom Tours (tel. 809/425–0099) arranges personalized tours for one to four persons at a cost of U.S.$25 per hour (minimum four hours). Staff members determine your particular interests (such as gardens, plantation houses, swimming at secluded beaches), pack a picnic lunch, and drive you in their own cars. They offer a familiarization tour for first-time visitors and often can take you to places that aren't normally open to the public. Ask for Margaret Leacock, the owner.

Getting Around

Taxis   Taxis operate at a fixed rate (BDS$30 for the first hour, less after that); settle the rate before you start off, and be sure you agree on whether it's in U.S. or Barbados dollars. Most drivers will cheerfully narrate a tour, though the noise

American Express offers Travelers Cheques built for two.

American Express® Cheques *for Two*. The first Travelers Cheques that allow either of you to use them because both of you have signed them. And only one of you needs to be present to purchase them.

Cheques *for Two* are accepted anywhere regular American Express Travelers Cheques are, which is just about everywhere. So stop by your bank, AAA* or any American Express Travel Service Office and ask for Cheques *for Two*.

AMERICAN EXPRESS Travelers Cheques ®

of the car may make it difficult for you to follow a rambling commentary colored with Bajan inflections.

Buses Public buses along Highway 1, St. James Road, are cheap (BDS$1.50, exact change appreciated), plentiful, reliable, and usually packed. The buses provide a great opportunity to experience local color, and your fellow passengers will be eager to share their knowledge.

Rental Cars It's a pleasure to explore Barbados by car, provided you take the time to study a good map and don't mind asking directions frequently. The more remote roads are in good repair, yet few are well lighted at night, and night falls quickly—at about 6 PM. Even in full daylight, the tall sugarcane fields lining a road can create near-zero visibility. Yet local residents are used to pointing travelers in the right direction, and some confused but intelligent drivers have been known to flag a passing taxi and pay to follow it back to a city area. Use caution: Pedestrians are everywhere. And remember, traffic keeps to the left throughout the island.

To rent a car you must have an international driver's license, obtainable at the airport and major car-rental firms for $5 if you have a valid driver's license. More than 40 offices rent minimokes for upwards of $45 a day plus insurance (about $215 a week), usually with a three-day or four-day minimum; cars with automatic shift are $45–$55 a day, or approximately $285 a week. Gas costs just over BDS$1 a liter (about $2 a gallon) and is extra. The speed limit, in keeping with the pace of life, is 37 miles per hour (60 kilometers per hour) in the country, 21 miles per hour in town. Operating a motorbike also requires an international driver's license—and some skill and daring.

The principal car-rental firms are **National** (tel. 809/426–0603), **Dear's Garage** on the south coast (tel. 809/429–9277 or 809/427–7853), **Sunny Isle** in Worthing (tel. 809/428–8009 or 809/428–2965), and **Sunset Crest Rentals** in St. James (tel. 809/432–1482). **P&S Car Rentals** (Spring Garden Hwy., tel. 809/424–2052) offers air-conditioned cars and jeeps with free customer delivery; it also arranges visitor driving permits.

Telephones and Mail

The area code for Barbados is 809. Except for emergency numbers, all phone numbers have seven digits and begin with 42 or 43.

An airmail letter from Barbados to the United States or Canada costs BDS95¢ per half ounce; an airmail postcard costs BDS65¢. Letters to the United Kingdom are BDS$1,10; postcards are BDS70¢.

Opening and Closing Times

Stores are open weekdays 8–4, Saturday 8–1. Some supermarkets remain open daily 8–6. Banks are open Monday to Thursday 9–3, Friday 9–1 and 3–5.

Dining

For the longest time, cuisine in the Caribbean was thought to be the weakest part of many an island vacation. In recent years, however, island visitors have come to realize that most of what they had been eating and complaining about was not Caribbean at all—just poorly prepared Continental fare garnished with a papaya slice or banana leaf. The cuisine of the islands is difficult to pin down because of the region's history as a colonial battleground and ethnic melting pot. The one quality that best defines Caribbean-style cooking has to be its essential spiciness. While reminiscent of Tex-Mex and Cajun, Caribbean cuisine is more varied and more subtle than its love of peppers implies. There is also the seafood that is unique to and abundant in the region. Another local favorite is conch, biologically quite close to land-loving escargots. Conch chowder, conch fritters, conch salad, conch cocktail—no island menu would be complete without at least a half-dozen conch dishes.

For many vacationers, much of the Caribbean experience has to do with the consumption of frothy blended fruit drinks, whose main and potent ingredient is Caribbean rum. Whether you are staying in a superdeluxe resort or a small, locally operated guest house, you will find that rum flows as freely as water.

After each restaurant review, we have indicated only when reservations are necessary or suggested. Since dining is usually casual, we have mentioned attire only when formal attire is needed.

Lodging

Plan ahead and reserve a room well before you travel to the Caribbean. If you have reservations but expect to arrive later than 5 or 6 PM, advise the hotel, inn, or guest house in advance. Unless so advised, some places will not hold your reservations after 6 PM. Also, be sure to find out what the rate quoted includes—use of sports facilities and equipment, airport transfers, and the like—and whether it operates on the European Plan (EP, with no meals), Continental Plan (CP, with Continental breakfast), Breakfast Plan (BP, with full hot breakfast), Modified American Plan (MAP, with two meals), or Full American Plan (FAP, with three meals), or is All-inclusive (with three meals, all facilities, and drinks unless otherwise noted). At the end of each review, we have listed the meal plans that the hotel offers. Not all plans are offered all-year round. Be sure to bring your deposit receipt with you in case any questions arise when you arrive at your hotel.

A Full American Plan may be ideal for travelers on a budget who don't want to worry about additional expenses; but travelers who enjoy a different dining experience each night will prefer to book rooms on a European Plan. Since many hotels insist on a Modified American Plan, particularly during the high season, find out whether you can exchange dinners for lunch.

Credit Cards

The following credit card abbreviations have been used: AE, American Express; D, Discover Card; DC, Diners Club; MC, MasterCard; V, Visa. It's a good idea to call ahead to check current credit card policies.

2 Portrait of Barbados

The Legacy of "Little England"

By John Wickham

The Caribbean of the 17th and 18th centuries has been described as the cockpit of European rivalry. The many wars and struggles between England and France and Holland and Spain for control of the Caribbees have left behind them much that has made the region one of the most interesting and colorful cultural laboratories in the world.

Although as a geographical region the Caribbean Islands share a common heritage, each island has developed its own personality, its own microculture distinguishing it from its neighbors. Visitors from Europe or North America expecting to find 'the islands' unified are often amazed at the diversity they encounter. Differences in the length and nature of the colonial overlordship and tutelage, in the landscape, in the nuances of language, religion, and architecture have produced a rich variety of accents, attitudes, styles of cooking, and building.

Similarities may be found among most of the islands in the Eastern Caribbean—the Windwards and the Leewards. However, the Barbados culture differs significantly from that of the other islands in that it reflects the effect of the British presence on the island for more than three centuries. The introduction of slaves from Africa was the main challenge to the British influence. Whereas other islands changed hands—some of them several times as a consequence of treaties and transfers negotiated on the other side of the Atlantic—Barbados remained staunchly British until 1966 when the island became an independent self-governing state within the Commonwealth.

So it is no wonder that the tiny island of 166 square miles has been called the Singular Island. Its singularity begins with the circumstances of its settlement: It is probably the only island in the chain that wasn't 'discovered' by Christopher Columbus. The first European settlers landing in 1627 found an island uninhabited but for a herd of wild pigs, the lineal descendants of a pair that had been left on the island 100 years earlier by some Portuguese sailors who had stopped for water on their way to Brazil.

The first settlers were English and they began a long tradition. Examples of the enduring British presence include cricket, place names such as Hastings, Worthing, a road called Chelsea, a square called Trafalgar and a parliament, which in 1989 celebrates 350 years of uninterrupted existence.

These residual pieces of evidence are only the outward and visible signs. Behind them lie the hardier substrata of three centuries of cultural influence, more enduring because less obvious, more subtle, and therefore less liable to eradication.

Barbados's gentle undulations are reminiscent of the English West Country and the Barbados accent is an heirloom of Gloucestershire and the West Country brogue of Somerset. The plantation house, the parish church, and the villagers, touching their caps to the gentry after the morning service all bear a resemblance to the English lord-of-the-manor, village green atmosphere.

The Barbados education system of elementary and secondary schools owes its existence to the presence of the Anglican Church and the influence of the clergy. The parson was, in a most Dickensian way, the chief cook and bottle-washer in the system. He managed the vestries, performed the functions of local government. He was also the chairman of the school board, with an authoritarian voice in decisions.

The system of secondary education, with its early emphasis on Latin and Greek, was an exported carbon copy of the English style of public (private) school. Harrison College, the oldest of these schools, was established by a wealthy sugar planter in 1733. More than 200 years later, its English headmaster would, on annual speech days, be certain to receive loud applause from the parents of pupils for his favorite comparison of the College examination results with those of the best English public schools.

The legal and parliamentary systems and, often the laws themselves, are faithful to their origins in the English systems.

Three years ago English historians from Somerset in search of linguistic connections with Barbados were struck by the strong burr of West Country accent to be found in the Martin's Bay area of the east coast of Barbados. Author Frank A. Collymore was moved to call Barbados

> this land where
> Sedgemoor sleeps beside the Guinea
> Coast . . .
> This land where Africa and Britain meet
> In exile, living apart but yet
> Mingling in haphazard and experimental
> union . . .
> . . . this land
> Often referred to as Little England.

Language and the tribal references of names and buildings are not only the conduits of the inheritance. They are also expressions of the thought and spirit of the original. For this reason they are the most reliable evidence of a cultural presence. Long after the people themselves have disappeared, the accent, the words, the manner of speaking remain.

The fact that vestiges of the old-time English language remain in living currency after 300 years is the most convincing argument for the endurance of the English influence. In his notes for a *Glossary of Words and Phrases of Barbados*, Frank Collymore draws attention to a sizeable array of words still extant in the Barbadian vocabulary, which have long since vanished from the English one. Who outside of a Shakespearian character, or an elderly Barbadian, uses the word 'handsel' for the first sale of the day, or 'a body' for a person, as in 'gin a body meets a body'? And who now 'keeps a noise' instead of making it, and refers to the wedge or block placed against a wheel to prevent its moving as a 'scotch'? A tot is still a tin cup and a scrip is still used to mean a small scrap of writing in Barbados.

Political independence, which has been a feature of the development of the English-speaking colonies in the 1960s, has had the effect of loosening the ties with Britain. The migrations of Barbadians during and shortly after the Second World War have come to an end with the establishing of restrictive legislation in what was once, fondly but sincerely, regarded as the Mother Country. The expatriate British civil servant is a phenomenon of the past and the Union Jack no longer flies at the mastheads of government buildings, nor do winners of island scholarships any longer regard the English and Scottish universities as the only repositories of higher education.

The geography that placed the islands in between the Americas has begun to exert its logic and Barbados, like other British dependencies, now feels the influence of the United States, and finds the memory of British dominance fading. But it will be a long time before the British presence disappears as the cultural roots are firmly grounded in 300 years of British heritage.

3 Cruising in Barbados

Cruising the Caribbean is perhaps the most relaxed and convenient way to tour this beautiful part of the world. A cruise offers all the benefits of island-hopping without the inconvenience. For example, a cruise passenger packs and unpacks only once and is not bound by flight schedules, tour-bus schedules, and "nonschedules" of fellow travelers.

Cruise ships usually call at several Caribbean ports on a single voyage. Thus, a cruise passenger experiences and savors the mix of nationalities and cultures of the Caribbean, as well as the variety of sightseeing opportunities, the geographic and topographic characteristics, and the ambience of each of the islands. A cruise passenger tries out each island on his or her cruise itinerary and has the opportunity to select favorites for in-depth discovery on a later visit.

Most vessels spend the morning or afternoon in port; others may linger longer. Almost all ships sell shore excursions at an extra cost, ranging from bus tours of the island to beach parties and scuba diving certifications. You can also arrange to participate in a variety of sporting activities during your stopover—just check with your ship's shore excursion director.

As a vacation, a cruise offers total peace of mind. All important decisions are made long before boarding the ship. The itinerary is set in advance, and the costs are known ahead of time and are all-inclusive, with no additional charge for meals, accommodations, entertainment, or recreational activities. (Only tips, shore excursions, and shopping are extra.) A cruise ship is a floating Caribbean resort. For details beyond the basics, given below, see *Fodor's Cruises and Ports of Call 1994*.

When to Go

Cruise ships sail from Barbados year-round—the waters are almost always calm, and the breezes keep temperatures fairly steady. Tropical storms are most likely September through November, but navigational equipment warns ships well in advance of impending foul weather, and, when necessary, cruise lines vary their itineraries to avoid storms.

Cruises are in high demand—and therefore also higher priced—during the standard vacation times in midsummer to early fall and around Easter. Some very good bargains are usually available during the immediate postvacation periods such as fall to mid-December, early spring, and the first few weeks after the Christmas and New Year's holidays. Christmas sailings are usually quite full and are priced at a premium.

Choosing Your Cruise

Cruise Information

Magazines *Cruises & Tours* profiles new ships and covers ports and itineraries; $11.80 per year for four issues (Vacation Publishers, 1502 Augusta St., Suite 415, Houston, TX 77057, tel. 713/974–6903).

Cruise Travel Magazine has photos and features on ships and ports of call. $9.97 per year for six issues (Box 342, Mt. Morris, IL 61054, tel. 815/734–4151 or 800/877–5983).

Newsletters *Cruise Digest Reports* has detailed ship reports, evaluations and ratings, and cruise industry news; $35 per year for six issues (1521 Alton Rd., Suite 350, Miami Beach, FL 33139, tel. 305/374–2224).

The Millegram is a newsletter with information on new ships, shipbuilding contracts, and changes in itineraries; $10 per year for four issues (Bill Miller Cruises Everywhere, Box 1463, Secaucus, NJ 07096, tel. 201/348–9390).

Ocean & Cruise News is a newsletter that profiles a different ship each month (World Ocean & Cruise Liner Society, Box 92, Stamford, CT 06901).

Types of Ships

The bigger the ship, the more it can offer: a greater number of activities, public rooms, dining options; a broader range of entertainment; and, of course, more passengers—a boon if you're gregarious, a burden if you're not. Rates on large ships can be slightly lower; the newer megaships are significantly less expensive per passenger to operate. Some ships, though, are too unwieldy to dock in smaller ports, and passengers may be shuttled to shore in a tender (a small boat).

Smaller cruise ships offer intimacy; the crew may be more informal, the level of activity less intense. Small ships can often slip into tiny, shallow harbors and dock right at quayside. Small ships come in two versions: simple excursion vessels and ultraluxurious ships. The excursion vessels usually don't have such amenities as pools, theaters, casinos, or libraries, and cabins are almost always closetlike.

Small luxury ships, which usually carry up to 200 passengers, have all the big-ship amenities, all-outside suites, and an exacting level of personalized service.

In considering size, don't forget to factor in other variables. Below, individual ship reviews show the passenger/crew ratio (or service ratio), which indicates how many passengers each crew member must serve. A service ration of 2:1 indicates that there's a crew member for every two passengers. All things being equal, choose the ship with the lower service ratio.

Space ratio, which indicates the relative size of cabins and public areas, is also very important. Divide a ship's gross tonnage by its passenger capacity to find this. A 25,000-ton vessel carrying 1,000 passengers will have a 25:1 space ratio. By industry standards, a ratio of 45:1 or above is considered spacious. Vessels with ratios under 25:1 can feel a bit like floating cans of sardines.

Also, study carefully a ship's on-board facilities. Is there a pool? How many entertainment lounges and movie theaters? How well equipped is the library or the health club? Facilities vary greatly.

Mainstream Ships These ships carry between 700 and 2,000 passengers and are similar to self-contained, all-inclusive resorts. You'll find pools, spas and saunas, movie theaters, exercise rooms, Las Vegas-style entertainment, a casino, and shore excursions, not to mention plenty of planned group activities.

The per diem is the daily rate, per passenger, when two persons share a cabin. Differences in ships, cabin categories, itineraries, and discounts, however, can skew that figure.

Within the mainstream cruise ship category, there are several subcategories: standard, premium, and luxury. The per diem listed with each one is based on a standard outside cabin in peak season—this being any ship's middle-of-the-road accommodation. Inside cabins have lower fares; fancy suites, with verandas or VCRs, cost more.

Luxury   Here you'll savor the finest cuisine afloat, dining at single seatings and by special order, and unusually large cabins. Most cabins are outside; some have verandas. These ships have high service and space ratios and extremely personalized service. Passengers are experienced and sophisticated cruisers. Evenings are dressy, with some formal occasions. You'll find fewer families and more seniors. **Per diem:** $300–$800.

Premium   Most ships fall into this category. They are run by highly experienced cruise lines, and you can expect competent, consistently professional service and entertainment and above-average itineraries. Waiters are apt to be of one nationality, adding a distinctive flair to the dining room. Hours and room service selection are better, the menu choice and quality of food higher, than those of the standard class. Featured dishes may be prepared tableside, and you're often able, with advance notice, to place special orders. Evenings are dressier, and the ambience similar to that of a good restaurant. There are usually a couple of formal nights. **Per diem:** $260–$590.

Standard   Menus are probably not extensive, and the food good but not extraordinary. Dress is more casual. Some of these ships are older, refitted vessels lacking modern amenities and state-of-the-art facilities. Others are gleaming new 60,000-ton megaships, carrying more than 2,000 passengers, that have been patterned after all-inclusive resorts where everything, from staff members to cabins to public spaces, seem rather impersonal. **Per diem:** $200–$410.

Cost

For one all-inclusive price (plus tips, shopping, bar bills, and other incidentals), you can have what many have called the trip of a lifetime. The axiom "the more you pay, the more you get" doesn't always hold true: Most mainstream ships are one-class vessels on which the passengers in the cheapest inside cabin eats the same food, sees the same shows, and shares the same amenities as one paying more than $1,000 per day for the top suite. (A notable exception is the *Queen Elizabeth 2*, where your dining-room assignment is based on your per diem. To some, a larger cabin—used principally for sleeping, showering, and changing clothes is not worth the extra money. Where price does make a difference is in the choice of ship.

A handy way to compare costs is to look at the per diem cost—the price of a cruise on a daily basis for each passenger, when two people occupy one cabin. In other words, if a seven-day cruise costs $700 per person, then the per diem for each person is $100. To select a cruise you can afford, consider the following elements.

Pre- and post-cruise arrangements: If you plan to arrive a day or two early at the port of embarkation, or linger a few days for sightseeing afterward, estimate the cost of your hotel, meals, car rental, sightseeing, and other expenditures. Cruise lines sell packages for pre- and post-cruise stays that can include hotel accommodations, transportation, tours, and extras such as car rentals, and some meals. These packages can cost less than similar stays you arrange on your own, but comparison shopping may reveal that you can do better on your own.

Airfare: Airfare and transfers are often included in the basic cruise fare; however, the cruise line chooses your airline and flight. Lines give an air transportation credit of $200–$400 for passengers who make their own arrangements. You may find a better airfare or more convenient routing, or use frequent-flyer miles.

Pretrip incidentals: These may include trip or flight insurance, the cost of boarding your pets, airport or port parking, depeature tax, visas, long-distance calls home, clothing, film or video-tape, and other miscellaneous expenses.

Shore excursions/expenses: Estimate an average of $70–$140 per passenger on a seven-day cruise.

Amusement and gambling allowances: Losses at bingo, in the casino, or in other forms of gambling, plus the cost of video games, can set you back a bundle. Of course, this is an entirely avoidable expense, but if you plan to bet, plan to lose. You must be over 18 to gamble on a cruise ship.

Shopping: Include what you expect to spend both for inexpensive souvenirs and major duty-free purchases.

On-board incidentals: According to the Cruise Lines International Association (CLIA), the typical tip total works out to $7–$11 per passenger per day. Daily onboard expenditures, including bar tabs, wine with meals, laundry, beauty parlor services, and gift shop purchases, average about $22.50 per person.

Accommodations

Where you sleep matters only if you enjoy extra creature comforts and are willing to pay for them; on most of today's one-class cruise ships no particular status or stigma is attached to your choice of cabin. Having said that, there's certainly an advantage to selecting the best cabin within your budget personally, rather than allowing your travel agent or cruise line representative to book you into the next available accommodation. Also, the earlier you book, the better the selection.

Cabin Size The term "stateroom," used on some ships, is usually interchangeable with cabin. Price is directly proportional to size and location. Also, the earlier you book, the better the selection.

Suites are the roomiest and best-equipped accommodations, even on the same ship they may differ in size, facilities, and prices. Most have a sitting area with a sofa and chairs; some have two bathrooms, occasionally with a whirlpool bathtub. The most expensive suites may be priced without regard to the number of passengers occupying them.

Furnishings Almost all modern cabins are equipped with individually controlled air-conditioning and a private bathroom—usually closet-size, with a toilet, small shower, and washbasin. More expensive cabins, especially on newer ships, may have a bathtub. Most cabins also have limited closet space, a small desk or dresser, a reading light, and, on many ships, a phono and TV, sometimes even a VCR.

Depending upon the ship and category, a cabin may have beds or berths. The beds may be twins, either side-by-side or at right angles. On many new ships, twin beds convert into a double. Lower-price cabins and cabins on smaller or older ships may have upper and lower bunks, or berths, especially when three or four people share the same accommodation. To provide more living space in the daytime, the room stewards fold the berths into the wall and frequently convert single beds into couches. More and more ships are reconfiguring their cabins to offer double beds; if that is what you want, get an assurance in writing that you have been assigned a cabin with a double bed.

Sharing Most cabins are designed for two people. If more than two people share a cabin, a substantial discount to the third or fourth person is usually offered. An additional discount is often offered for children sharing a cabin with their parents. When no single cabins are available, passengers traveling on their own must pay a single supplement, which usually ranges from 125% to 200% of the double-occupancy per person rate. On request, however, many cruise lines will match up two strangers of the same sex in a cabin at the double-occupancy rate.

Location On all ships, regardless of size or design, the bow (front) and stern (back) bounce up and down on the waves far more than amidships (middle). Similarly, the closer your deck is to the true center of the ship—about halfway between the bottom of the hull and the highest deck—the less you will feel the ship's movement. Some cruise lines charge more for cabins amidships; most charge more for the higher decks.

Outside cabins have portholes or windows (which cannot be opened); on the upper decks, the view from outside cabins may be partially obstructed by life-boats or look out onto a public deck. Because outside cabins are more desirable, many newer upscale and luxury ships are configured with outside cabins only. On a few ships more expensive outside cabins have a private veranda that opens onto the sea.

Inside cabins on older vessels are often smaller and oddly shaped in order to fit around the ship's particular configuration. On newer ships, the floor plans of inside cabins are virtually identical to those of outside cabins. If sleeping in windowless inside cabins doesn't make you feel claustrophobic, it's a great way to save money.

Cruise brochures show the ship's layout deck by deck and the approximate location and shape of every cabin and suite. Study the map to make sure the cabin you pick is not near the noise of public rooms or the ship's engine, and to make sure that you are near stairs or an elevator. If detailed layouts of typical cabins are printed, you can determine what kind of beds the cabin has, if it has a window or a porthole, and what furnishings are provided. Be aware that configurations within each category can differ.

Booking Your Cruise

Most cruise ships sail at or near capacity, especially during high season, so consider making reservations as much as two years in advance. On the other hand, you may be able to save hundreds of dollars by booking close to the sailing date, especially if you go through a cruise broker or a discounter.

Getting the Best Cruise for Your Dollar

It used to be an article of faith that one travel agent would give you cruise rates identical to those offered by any other. In fact, until airline deregulation in 1978, it was illegal for travel agents to discount the set price for airline tickets. And by custom, most other bookings—from cruise ships to hotels to car rentals—were also sold at the same price, regardless of the agency. The rare discount or rebate was kept discreetly under the table. In recent years, however, this practice among travel agencies has gradually declined—and cruise travelers benefit.

Like everything in retail, each cruise has a *list* price. However, the actual selling price can vary tremendously: These days, if you ask any 10 passengers on almost any given ship what they're paying per diem, they'll give you 10 sharply different answers. Discounts on the same accommodation can range from 5% on a single fare to 50% on a second fare in a cabin. Approach deep discounts with skepticism. Fewer than a dozen cabins may be offered at the discounted price, they may be inside cabins, and the fare may not include air transportation or transfer.

Though a single, sure-fire path to whopping savings may not exist, you can maximize your chances in several ways:

Full-Service Travel Agents Consider booking with a full-service travel agent. He or she can make your arrangements and deal direclty with airlines, cruise companies, car-rental agencies, hotels, and resorts. You won't be charged a service fee—agents make money on commissions from the cruise lines and other suppliers—and you'll eliminate such expenses as long-distance phone calls and postage. Some good agents throw in complimentary flight bags and champagne.

However, don't rely solely on your agent when selecting your cruise. Since most travel agencies book everything from cruises to business flights to theme-park vacations, your local agent may not possess a full knowledge of the cruise industry. Agents may have sailed on some of the ships and seen some ports, but most have acquired their knowledge of competing cruise lines from the same booklets and brochures available to the public. Because agents work on commission, there is some potential conflict of interest. Fortunately, reputable agents remain relatively unbiased.

Cruise-Only Travel Agencies "Cruise-only" travel agencies constitute one of the fastest growing segments of the travel industry, and most major towns or cities have at least one or two. Their knowledgeable employees may have sailed on many of these ships themselves. But that's only one of their strengths. Working in conjunction with specific cruise lines, cruise-only agencies obtain significant discounts by agreeing to sell large blocks of tickets. To make their quotas, they pass along savings to their clients. The discount you get depends on agency, cruise line, season, the ship's popularity, and current demand.

Cruise Travel Clubs Some cruise-only agencies are run as private clubs, and for an annual fee of $25 to $50 offer members a newsletter, flight bags or other free gifts, special benefits to repeat clients, and sometimes, if the agency negotiates a group charter with the cruise lines, better rates.

Haggling Shopping around may or may not get you a better deal. A number of cruise-only travel agencies discount every cruise they sell—one agency may sell at fixed prices, while another may charge whatever supply and demand will allow. Even when an agent quotes a particular price, go ahead and ask for a further discount. You have absolutely nothing to lose. If you don't ask for the lowest price, you're probably not going to get it. On the other hand, this ploy is best used by experienced cruisers who know what they're looking for. Beginners may find it's worth paying a little more for the sound advice an experienced agent may offer.

Last-Minute Booking When cruise companies have cancellations or unsold cabins, they use cruise-only agencies and cruise specialists to recoup revenue. The closer it is to the sailing date, the bigger the savings. Typically, discounts range from 25% to more than 60%. To obtain the best discount, you can't book very far in advance (usually only from two weeks to a month) and you have to be flexible— ideally prepared to leave on as little as 24 hours' notice. You might end up spending your vacation at home, or you might luck into the travel bargain of a lifetime.

A caveat: Cabin choice is limited, air transportation may not be included, and you may not get the meal seating you prefer. Also, think about why those cabins haven't been sold. Do you want to sail for less on the leftovers, or pay more to sail on a ship that is consistently full because it is consistently good?

Early Booking Several cruise lines have recently begun offering discounts to customers who book early. In addition to the discount, an early booking gives you a better choice of cabin and sailing date. Some lines guarantee that passengers who book early will receive any lower rate that the line subsequently posts on that particular cruise. Some lines offer an additional discount for paying the full fare in advance.

Swindlers Always be on the lookout for a scam. Though reputable agencies far outnumber crooks, a handful of marketeers use deceptive and unethical tactics. The best way to avoid being fleeced is to deal with an agency that has been in business for at least five years. If you have any doubts about its credibility, consult your local Better Business Bureau or consumer protection agency before you mail in any deposits. Be wary of bait-and-switch tactics: If you are told that an advertised bargain cruise is sold out, *do not* be persuaded to book a more expensive substitute. Also, if you are told that your cruise reservation was canceled due to overbooking and that you must pay extra for a confirmed rescheduled sailing, demand a full refund. Finally, if ever you fail to receive a voucher or ticket on the promised date, place an inquiry immediately.

Choosing the Right Agency or Club How do you find an honest, competent travel agent? Word of mouth is always a safe bet—get recommendations from friends, family, and colleagues, especially those who have cruised before. Or look in the Yellow Pages for agents identified as members of "CLIA" (Cruise Lines International Association) or "ASTA" (American Society of Travel Agents). In theory, there's little difference between the level of service you'll receive from a tiny mom-and-pop agency and a national chain. In practice, however, larger, well-established agencies are more likely to employ experienced cruisers, and smaller agencies may give you more personal attention. Check around and weigh your options carefully.

Then phone for an appointment to interview a few prospects. Choose the agent who takes a personal interest in finding the right cruise line for you.

Videotapes

Most travel agencies have a library of travel tapes, including some on specific cruise ships; usually you can also borrow, rent, or buy tapes directly from the cruise line. As you view the tape, keep in mind that the cruise company made this tape to show its ship to the best advantage. Still, you will get a visual idea of the size and shape of the cabins, dining room, swimming pool, and public rooms; the kinds of attractions, amenities, and entertainment on board; and the ports and islands at which you'll stop.

You can also obtain VHS or Beta videos about many cruises and cruise ships from **Vacations on Video** (1309 E. Northern St., Phoenix, AZ 85020, tel. 602/483–1551; about $20 per tape). **Vacations Ashore & All the Ships at Sea** (173 Minuteman Causeway, Cocoa Beach, FL 32931, tel. 407/868–2131; $90 per year or $25 per issue), a bimonthly video magazine, reviews five ships per issue.

Cruise Brochures

Although a brochure is as promotional as a videotape, it can provide valuable information about a ship and what it has to offer. Make sure the brochures you select are the most recently published versions: Schedules, itineraries, and prices change constantly. Study the maps of the decks and cabin layouts, and be sure to read the fine print to find out just what you'll be getting for your money. Check out the details on fly/cruise programs; optional pre- and post-cruise packages; the ship's credit card and check-cashing policy; embarkation and debarkation procedures; and legal matters of payment, cancellation, insurance, and liability.

Payment

Deposit Most cruises must be reserved with a refundable deposit of $200–$500 per person, depending upon how expensive the cruise is; the balance is to be paid one to two months before you sail. Don't let a travel agent pressure you into paying a larger deposit or paying the balance earlier. If the cruise is less than a month away, however, it may be legitimate for the agency to require to pay the entire amount immediately.

If possible, pay your deposit and balance via credit card. This gives you some recourse if you need to cancel, and you can ask the credit card company to intercede on your behalf in case of problems. Don't forget to get a receipt.

Handing money over to your travel agent constitutes a contract, so before you pay your deposit, study the cruise brochure to find out the provisions of the cruise contract. What is the payment schedule and cancellation policy? Will there be any additional charges before you can board your ship, such as transfers, port fees, local taxes, or baggage charges? If your air connection requires you to spend an evening in a hotel near the port before or after the cruise, is there an extra cost?

Cancellation If you cancel your reservation 45–60 days prior to your scheduled cruise (the grace period varies from line to line), you may receive your entire deposit or payment back. You will forfeit some or even all of your deposit if you cancel any closer to cruise time. In rare cases, however, if your reason for canceling is unavoidable, the cruise line may decide, as its discretion, to waive some or all of the forfeiture. An average cancellation charge would be $100 one month before sailing, $100 plus 50% of the ticket price 15–30 days before sailing, and $100 plus 75% of the ticket price between 14 days and 24 hours before sailing. If you simply fail to show up when the ship sails, you will lose the entire amount you've paid. Many travel agents also assess a small cancellation fee. Check their policy.

Insurance Cruise lines sell cancellation insurance for about $50 per ticket (the amount varies according to the line, the number of days in the cruise, and the price you paid for the ticket). Such insurance protects you against cancellation fees; it may also reimburse you, on a deductible basis, if your luggage is lost or damaged. Note, however, that there are usually some restrictions. For instance, the trip cancellation policy may insure that you receive a full refund *only* if you cancel and notify the cruise line no less than 72 hours in advance. Some travel agencies and cruise clubs give customers free trip insurance; be sure to ask when booking your cruise.

Cruise Lines

To find out which ships are sailing where and when they depart, contact the **Caribbean Tourism Organization** (20 E. 46th St., 4th floor, New York, NY 10017, tel. 212/682–0435). The CTA carries up-to-date information about cruise lines that sail to its member nations. Full-service and cruise-only travel agencies are also a good source; they stock brochures and catalogues issued by most of the major lines and have the latest information about prices, departure dates, and itineraries. The **Cruise Lines International Association** (CLIA) publishes a useful pamphlet entitled "Cruising Answers to Your Questions"; to order a copy send a self-addressed business-size envelope with 52¢ postage to CLIA (500 5th Ave., Suite 1407, New York, NY 10110).

A complete list of cruise lines that operate in the Caribbean appears below.

American Canadian Caribbean Line (Box 368, Warren, RI 02885, tel. 401/247–0955 in Rhode Island or 800/556–7450).
Carnival Cruise Lines (3655 N.W. 87th Ave., Miami, FL 33178, tel. 800/327–9501).
Celebrity Cruises (5200 Blue Lagoon Dr., Miami, FL 33126, tel. 800/437–3111).
Clipper Cruise Line (7711 Bonhomme Ave., St. Louis, MO 63105, tel. 800/325–0010).
Club Med (40 W. 57th St., New York, NY 10019, tel. 800/CLUB–MED).
Commodore Cruise Line (800 Douglas Rd., Suite 700, Coral Gables, FL 33134, tel. 800/237–5361).
Costa Cruises (World Trade Center, 80 S.W. 8th St., Miami, FL 33130, tel. 800/462–6782).
Crown Cruise Line (Box 3000, 2790 N. Federal Hwy., Boca Raton, FL 33431, tel. 800/841–7447).

Crystal Cruises (2121 Ave. of the Stars, Los Angeles, CA 90067, tel. 800/446–6645).

Cunard (555 5th Ave., New York, NY 10017, tel. 800/221–4770).

Dolphin/Majesty Cruise Lines (901 South American Way, Miami, FL 33132, tel. 800/222–1003).

Fantasy Cruise Lines (5200 Blue Lagoon Dr., Miami, FL 33126, tel. 800/437–3111).

Holland America Line (300 Elliott Ave. W, Seattle, WA 98119, tel. 800/426–0327).

Norwegian Cruise Line (95 Merrick Way, Coral Gables, FL 33134, tel. 305/447–9660 or 800/327–7030).

Ocean Cruises (1510 S. E. 17th St., Fort Lauderdale, FL 33316, tel. 800/556–8850).

Premier Cruise Lines (Box 517, Cape Canaveral, FL 32920, tel. 800/327–7113).

Princess Cruises (10100 Santa Monica Blvd., Los Angeles, CA 90067, tel. 310/553–1770).

Regency Cruises (260 Madison Ave., New York, NY 10016, tel. 212/972–4499 or 800/388–5500).

Renaissance Cruises (1800 Eller Dr., Suite 300, Box 350307, Fort Lauderdale, FL 33335, tel. 800/525–2450).

Royal Caribbean Cruise Line (1050 Caribbean Way, Miami, FL 33132, tel. 800/327–6700).

Royal Cruise Line (1 Maritime Plaza, San Francisco, CA 94111, tel. 415/956–7200).

Royal Viking Line (Kloster Cruise Limited, 95 Merrick Way, Coral Gables, FL 33134, tel. 800/422–8000).

Seabourn Cruise Line (55 Francisco St., San Francisco, CA 94133, tel. 800/351–9595).

Seawind Cruise Line (1750 Coral Way, Miami, FL 33145, tel. 800/258–8006).

Sun Line Cruises (1 Rockefeller Plaza, Suite 315, New York, NY 10020, tel. 800/872–6400).

Windstar Cruises (300 Elliott Ave. W, Seattle, WA 98119, tel. 800/258–7245).

4 Exploring Barbados

The island's most popular sights and attractions can be seen comfortably in four or five excursions, each lasting one day or less. The five tours described here begin with Bridgetown and then cover central Barbados, the eastern shore, north-central Barbados, and the south shore. Before you set out in a car, minimoke, or taxi, ask at your hotel or the Board of Tourism for a free copy of the detailed Barbados Holiday Map and check performance or opening times.

Bridgetown

Numbers in the margin correspond to points of interest on the Bridgetown map.

Bridgetown is a bustling city, complete with rush hours and traffic congestion; you'll avoid hassle by taking the bus or a taxi. Sightseeing will take an hour or so, and the shopping areas are within walking distance.

In the center of town, overlooking the picturesque harbor known as the Careenage, is **Trafalgar Square,** with its impressive monument to Horatio, Lord Nelson. It predates the Nelson's Column in London's Trafalgar Square by about two decades (and for more than a century Bajans have petitioned to replace it with a statue of a Bajan). Here are also a war memorial and a three-dolphin fountain commemorating the advent of running water in Barbados in 1865.

Bridgetown is a major Caribbean free port. The principal shopping area is **Broad Street,** which leads west from Trafalgar Square past the House of Assembly and Parliament buildings. These Victorian Gothic structures, like so many smaller buildings in Bridgetown, stand beside a growing number of modern office buildings and shops. Small colonial buildings, their balconies trimmed with wrought iron, reward the visitor who has patience and an appreciative eye.

The water that bounds Trafalgar Square is called the **Careenage,** a finger of sea that made early Bridgetown a natural harbor and a gathering place. Here working schooners were careened (turned on their sides) to be scraped of barnacles and repainted. Today the Careenage

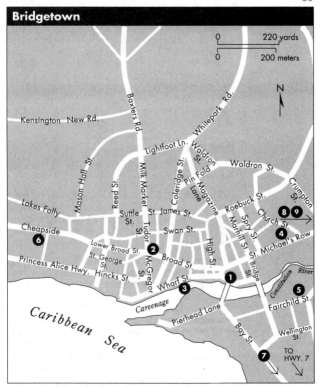

Bridgetown

0   220 yards
0   200 meters

N

Barbados
Museum, **7**

Broad Street, **2**

Careenage, **3**

Cheapside
Market, **6**

Fairchild
Market, **5**

Queen's Park, **8**

Queen's Park
House, **9**

St. Michael's
Cathedral, **4**

Trafalgar
Square, **1**

serves mainly as a berth for fiberglass pleasure yachts.

Although no one has proved it conclusively, George Washington, on his only visit outside the United States, is said to have worshiped at **St. Michael's Cathedral** east of Trafalgar Square. The structure was nearly a century old when he visited in 1751, and it has since been destroyed by hurricanes and rebuilt twice, in 1780 and 1831.

The two bridges over the Careenage are the Chamberlain Bridge and the Charles O'Neal Bridge, both of which lead to Highway 7 and south to the **Fairchild Market.** On Saturdays the activity there and at the **Cheapside Market** (on the north end of Lower Broad Street, across from St. Mary's Church Square) recall the lively days before the coming of the supermarket and the mall, when the outdoor markets of Barbados were the daily heart and soul of shopping and socializing.

About a mile south of Bridgetown on Highway 7, the unusually interesting **Barbados Museum** has artifacts and mementos of military history and everyday life in the 19th century. Here you'll see cane-harvesting implements, lace wedding dresses, ancient (and frightening) dentistry instruments, and slave sale accounts kept in a spidery copperplate handwriting. Wildlife and natural-history exhibits, a well-stocked gift shop, and a good café are also here, in what used to be the military prison. *Hwy. 7, Garrison Savannah, tel. 809/427–0201. Admission: BDS$7. Open Mon.–Sat. 10–6.*

East of St. Michael's Cathedral, **Queen's Park,** now being restored to its original splendor, is home to one of the largest trees in Barbados: an immense baobab more than 10 centuries old. The historic **Queen's Park House,** former home of the commander of the British troops, has been converted into a theater—with an exhibition room on the lower floor—and a restaurant. Queen's Park is a long walk from Trafalgar Square or the museum; you may want to take a taxi. *Open daily 9–5.*

Central Barbados

Numbers in the margin correspond to points of interest on the Barbados map.

(10) For nervous swimmers, the most interesting place for getting into the water is the **Folkstone Underwater Park,** north of Holetown. While Folkstone has a land museum of marine life, the real draw is the underwater snorkeling trail around Dottin's Reef, with glass-bottom boats available for use by nonswimmers. A dredge barge sunk in shallow water is the home to myriad fish, and it and the reef are popular with scuba divers. Huge sea fans, soft coral, and the occasional giant turtle are sights to see.

(11) Highway 2 will take you to **Harrison's Cave.** These pale-gold limestone caverns, complete with subterranean streams and waterfalls, are entirely organic and said to be unique in the Caribbean. Open since 1981, the caves are so extensive that tours are made by electric tram (hard hats are provided, but all that may fall on you is a little dripping water). *Tel. 809/438–6640. Admission: BDS$15 adults, BDS$7.50 children. Reservations recommended. Open daily 9–4.*

(12) The nearby **Welchman Hall Gully,** a part of the National Trust in St. Thomas, affords another ideal opportunity to commune with nature. Here are acres of labeled flowers and trees, the occasional green monkey, and great peace and quiet. *Tel. 809/438–6671. Admission: BDS$5 adults, BDS$2.50 children. Open daily 9–5.*

(13) Continue along Highway 2 to reach the **Flower Forest,** 8 acres of fragrant flowering bushes, canna and ginger lilies, and puffball trees. Another hundred species of flora combine with the tranquil views of Mt. Hillaby to induce in visitors what may be a relaxing and very pleasant light-headedness. *Tel. 809/433–8152. Admission: BDS$10. Open daily 9–5.*

(14) Go back toward Bridgetown and take Highway 4 and smaller roads to **Gun Hill** for a view so pretty it seems almost unreal: Shades of green and gold cover the fields all the way to the horizon, the picturesque gun tower is surrounded by brilliant flowers, and the white limestone lion behind the garrison is a famous landmark. Military invalids were once sent here to convalesce. *No phone. Admission: BDS$5 adults, BDS$2.50 children.*

The Eastern Shore

Take Highway 3 across the island to Bathsheba and the phenomenal view from the **Atlantis,** one of the oldest hotels in Barbados, where you may need help getting up from the table after sampling the lunch buffet.

⑮ In the nearby **Andromeda Gardens** (tel. 809/433–9261), a fascinating small garden set into the cliffs overlooking the sea, are unusual and beautiful plant specimens from around the world, collected by the late horticulturist Iris Bannochie and now administered by the Barbados National Trust. *Tel. 809/433–1524. Admission: BDS$10. Open daily 9–5.*

⑯ North of Bathsheba, **Barclay's Park** offers a similar view and picnic facilities in a wooded seafront area. At the nearby **Chalky Mount Potteries,** you'll find craftspersons making and selling their wares.

A drive north to the isolated Morgan Lewis Beach (*see* Beaches in Chapter 5) or to Gay's Cove, which every Bajan calls Cove Bay, will put
⑱ you in reach of the town of **Pie Corner.** Pie Corner is known not for baked goods but for artifacts left by the Caribe and Arawak tribes who once lived here.

⑲ The **Animal Flower Cave** at North Point, reached by Highway 1B, displays small sea anemones, or seaworms, that resemble jewellike flowers as they open their tiny tentacles. For a small fee you can explore inside the cavern and see the waves breaking just outside it. *Tel. 809/439–8797. Admission: BDS$3 adults, BDS$1.50 children under 12. Open daily 9–5.*

North-Central Barbados

The attractions of north-central Barbados may well be combined with the tour of the eastern shore.

Barbados

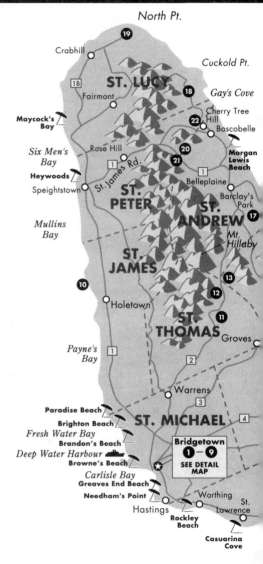

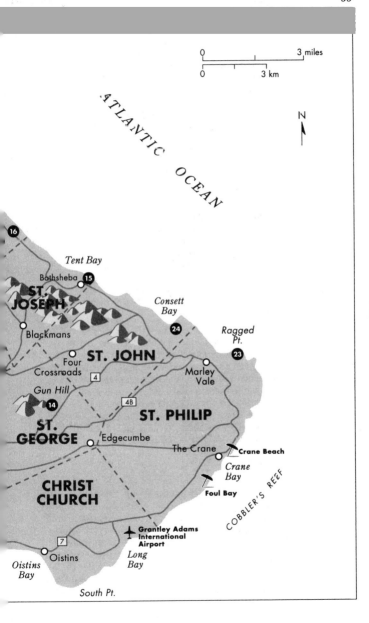

0 _____ 3 miles

0 _____ 3 km

N

ATLANTIC OCEAN

16

Tent Bay

Bathsheba **15**

ST. JOSEPH

Consett Bay

Blackmans

24

Ragged Pt.

ST. JOHN

23

Four Crossroads

4

Marley Vale

Gun Hill

4B

14

ST. PHILIP

ST. GEORGE

Edgecumbe

The Crane ☂ Crane Beach

Crane Bay

CHRIST CHURCH

☂ Foul Bay

COBBLER'S REEF

7

✈ Grantley Adams International Airport

Oistins

Long Bay

Oistins Bay

South Pt.

20 The **Barbados Wildlife Reserve** can be reached on Highway 1 from Speightstown on the west coast. Here are herons, land turtles, a kangaroo, screeching peacocks, innumerable green monkeys and their babies doing all manner of things, geese, brilliantly colored parrots, and a friendly otter. The fauna are not in cages, so step carefully and keep your hands to yourself. The preserve has been much improved in recent years with the addition of a giant walk-in aviary and natural-history exhibits. Terrific photo opportunities are everywhere. *Tel. 809/422–8826. Admission: BDS$10 adults, BDS$5 children under 12 with adult. Open daily 10–5.*

21 Just to the south is **Farley Hill,** a national park in northern St. Peter Parish; the rugged landscape explains why they call this the Scotland area. Gardens; lawns; gigantic mahogany, whitewood, and casuarina trees; and an avenue of towering royal palms surround the imposing ruins of a once magnificent plantation great house. Partially rebuilt for the filming of *Island in the Sun*, the structure was later destroyed by fire. *Admission: BDS$2 per car; walkers free. Open daily 8:30–6.*

22 **St. Nicholas Abbey** near Cherry Tree Hill, named for a former owner and the oldest (c. 1650) great house in Barbados, is well worth visiting for its stone-and-wood architecture in the Jacobean style. Fascinating home movies, made by the present owner's father, record scenes of Bajan town and plantation life in the 1920s and 1930s. There are no set showing times; you need only ask to see them. *Tel. 809/422–8725. Admission: $2.50. Open weekdays 10–3:30.*

The South Shore

Driving east on Highways 4 and 4B, you'll note the many **chattel houses** along the route; the property of tenant farmers, these ever-expandable houses were built to be dismantled and moved when necessary. On the coast, the appro-

23 priately named **Ragged Point Lighthouse** is where the sun first shines on Barbados and its dramatic Atlantic seascape. About 4 miles to the northwest, in the eastern corner of St. John Parish, the coralstone buildings and serenely beau-

㉔ tiful grounds of **Codrington Theological College,** founded in 1748, stand on a cliff overlooking Consett Bay.

Take the smaller roads southeast to reach **Marriott's Sam Lord's Castle** (*see* Lodging in Chapter 8), the Regency house built by the buccaneer. Most of the rooms are furnished with the fine antiques he is said to have acquired from passing ships (note the mahogany four-poster), but he had to hire Italian artisans to create the elaborate plaster ceilings. The tour is free to guests; others pay a small fee.

5 Sports, Fitness, Beaches

Participant Sports

Golfing

The Royal Westmoreland Golf and Country Club is still in its planning stages and until it is completed, golfers favor the 18 holes at the **Sandy Lane Club** (tel. 809/432–1145), whose dramatic 7th hole is famous both for its elevated tee and its incredible view. There is also a 9-hole course at the **Rockley Resort** (tel. 809/435–7873), and another 9 holes at **Heywoods** (tel. 809/422–4900). All are open (for various fees) to nonguests.

Hiking/Jogging

Hilly but not mountainous, the interior of Barbados is ideal for hiking. The **Barbados National Trust** (Belleville, St. Michael, tel. 809/436–9033) sponsors free walks year-round on Sunday, from 6:30 AM to about 9:30 AM and from 3:30 PM to 5:30 PM, as well as special moonlight hikes when the heavens permit. Newspapers announce the time and meeting place (or you can call the Trust).

Less serious (but great fun) is the **Hash House Harriers,** an international running group with relaxed jogging at different points each week. Contact John Carpenter (tel. 809/429–5151 days or 809/429–3818 evenings).

Horseback Riding

Reasonable prices ($17–$22) for one-hour trots, including hotel pickup, come from **Valley Hill Stables** (Christ Church, tel. 809/423–6180) and **Ye Old Congo Road Stables** (St. Philip, tel. 809/423–8293), which take riders through sugar plantations. On the west coast, **Brighton Stables** (tel. 809/425–9381) offers sunrise and sunset walks along beaches and palm groves.

Parasailing

Parasailing, during which you wear a parachute harness and take off from a raft as you're towed by a speedboat, is available, wind conditions permitting, on the beaches of St. James and Christ Church. Just ask at any hotel, then flag down a speedboat (though it may have found you first).

Squash

Squash courts can be reserved at the **Rockley Resort** (tel. 809/435–7880) and **Barbados Squash Club** (Marine House, Christ Church, tel. 809/427–7913).

Submarining

Submarines are enormously popular with families and those who enjoy watching fish without getting wet, and the 28-passenger *Atlantis* turns the Caribbean into a giant aquarium. The 45-minute trip takes you as much as 150 feet below the surface for a look at what even sport divers rarely see. The nighttime dives, using high-power searchlights, are spectacular. *Tel. 809/436–8929. Cost: $69.50 adults, $31.50 children 4–12.*

Tennis

Most hotels have tennis courts that can be reserved day and night. Be sure to bring your whites; appropriate dress is expected on the court.

Spectator Sports

Cricket

The island is mad for cricket, and you can sample a match at almost any time of year. While the season is June through late December, test matches are played in the first half of the year. The newspapers give the details of time and place.

Horse Racing

Horse racing takes place on alternate Saturdays, from January to May and from July to November, at the **Garrison Savannah** in Christ Church, about 3 miles south of Bridgetown. Appropriate dress might be described as "casual elegance." *Tel. 809/426–3980. Admission: BDS$10 adults, BDS$5 children under 12.*

Polo

Polo, the sport of kings, is played seriously in Barbados. Matches are held at the **Polo Club** in St. James on Wednesday and Saturday from September to March. Hang around the club room after the match. That's where the lies, the legends, and the invitations happen. *Admission: about $2.50.*

Rugby

The rough-and-tumble game of rugby is played at the Garrison Savannah; schedules are available from the **Barbados Rugby Club.** Contact Victor Roach (809/435–6543).

Soccer

The "football," or soccer, season runs from January through June; game schedules are available from the **Barbados Football Association** (tel. 809/424–4413).

Water Sports

Sailing and Fishing

Blue Jay Charters (tel. 809/422–2098) has a 45-foot, fully equipped fishing boat, with a crew that knows the waters where blue marlin, sailfish, barracuda, and kingfish play. Two other choices are **Sailing Charter Tiami Cruises** (tel. 809/425–5800) and *Carie-Dee,* a 36-foot private yacht (tel. 809/422–2319) that takes guests by the day or half day.

Scuba Diving

Diving is America's fastest-growing sport. While scuba (which stands for self-contained underwater breathing apparatus) looks and is surprisingly simple, *phone your physician before your vacation and make sure that you have no condition that should prevent you from diving!* Possibilities include common colds and other nasal infections, which can be worsened by diving, and ear infections, which can be worsened and cause underwater vertigo as well. Asthmatics can usually dive safely but must have their doctor's okay. A full checkup is an excellent idea, especially if you're over 30. Since it can be dangerous to travel on a plane after diving, you should schedule both your diving courses and travel plans accordingly.

At depths of below 30 feet, all sorts of physiological and chemical changes take place in the body in response to an increase in water pressure, so learning to dive with a reputable instructor is a must. Nitrogen, for example, which ordinarily escapes from the body through respiration, forms bubbles in the diver's bloodstream. If the diver resurfaces at a rate of more than one foot per second, these nitrogen bubbles may accumulate; the severe joint pains caused by this process are known as "the bends." If the nitrogen bubbles travel to your heart or brain, the result can be fatal.

In addition to training you how to resurface slowly enough, a qualified instructor can teach you to read "dive tables," the charts that calculate how long you can safely stay at certain depths.

The ideal way to learn this sport is to take a resort course once you've arrived at your Caribbean destination. The course will usually consist of two to three hours of instruction on land, with time spent in a swimming pool or waist-deep water to get used to the mouthpiece and hose (known as the regulator) and the mask. A shallow 20-foot dive from a boat or beach, supervised by the instructor, follows.

Successful completion of this introductory course may prompt you to earn a certification card—often called a C-card—from one of the major accredited diving organizations: NAUI (National Association of Underwater Instructors), CMAS (Confederation Mondiale des Activités Subaquatiques, which translates into World Underwater Federation), NASE (National Association of Scuba Educators), or PADI (Professional Association of Diving Instructors). PADI offers a free list of training facilities; write PADI for information (1251 E. Dyer Rd., #100, Santa Ana, CA 92705).

A certification course will keep you very busy and pleasantly tired for most of your vacation. If your travel plans include a great deal of sightseeing as well, you'll have little time left to relax. You may wish to complete the classroom instruction and basic skills training at your hometown YMCA, for example, then do your five required open-water dives on vacation.

Unfortunately, there are a few disreputable individuals who may try to assure you that they can teach you everything you need to know about diving even though they aren't certified instructors. DON'T BELIEVE IT! Reputable diving shops proudly display their association with the organizations mentioned above. If you have any doubt, ask to see evidence of accreditation. Legitimate instructors will happily show you their credentials and will insist on seeing *your* C-card before a dive.

Keep in mind that your presence can easily damage the delicate underwater ecology. By standing on the bottom you can break fragile coral that took centuries to grow. Many reefs are legally protected marine parks; spearfishing or taking living shells and coral is rude and destructive, and often strictly prohibited. When in doubt, remember the diver's caveat: "Take only pictures, leave only bubbles."

Barbados, with a rich and varied underwater world, is one of the few islands in the Caribbean that offer activity for both divers and nondivers. Many dive shops provide instruction (the three-hour beginner's "resort courses" and the week-long certification courses) followed by a shallow dive, usually on Dottin's Reef. Trained divers can explore reefs, wrecks, and the walls of "blue holes," the huge circular depressions in the ocean floor. Not to be missed by certified, guided divers is the *Stavronikita*, a 368-foot Greek freighter that was deliberately sunk at about 125 feet; hundreds of butterfly fish hang out around its mast, and the thin rays of sunlight that filter down through the water make exploring the huge ship a wonderfully eerie experience.

Dive Barbados (Watersports, Sunset Crest Beach, near Holetown, St. James Parish, tel.

809/432–7090) provides beginner's instruction (resort course) and reef and wreck dives with a friendly, knowledgeable staff. At **The Dive Shop, Ltd.** (Grand Barbados Beach Resort, tel. 809/426–9947), experienced divers can participate in deep dives to old wrecks to look for bottles and other artifacts (and you can usually keep what you find). **Willie's Watersports** (Heywoods Hotel, tel. 809/422–4900, ext. 2831) offers instruction and a range of diving excursions. **Exploresub Barbados** (Divi Southwinds Beach Resort, tel. 809/428–7181) operates a full range of daily dives. **Dive Boat Safari** (Barbados Hilton, tel. 809/427–4350) offers full diving and instruction services.

Snorkeling

Snorkeling requires no special skills, and most hotels that rent equipment have a staff member or, at the very least, a booklet offering instruction in snorkeling basics.

As with any water sport, it's never a good idea to snorkel alone, especially if you're out of shape. You don't have to be a great swimmer to snorkel, but occasionally currents come up that require stamina. The four dimensions as we know them seem altered underwater. Time seems to slow and stand still, so wear a water-resistant watch and let someone on land know when to expect you back. Your sense of direction may also fail you when you're submerged. Many a vacationer has ended up half a mile or more from shore—which isn't a disaster unless you're already tired, chilly, and it's starting to get dark.

Remember that taking souvenirs—shells, pieces of coral, interesting rocks—is forbidden. Many reefs are legally protected marine parks, where removal of living shells is prohibited because it upsets the ecology. Because it is impossible to tell a living shell from a dead one, the wisest course is simply not to remove any. Needless to say, underwater is also not the place to discard your cigarette packs, gum wrappers, or any other litter.

Good snorkel equipment isn't cheap, and you may not like the sport once you've tried it, so get some experience with rented equipment, which is always inexpensive, before investing in quality mask, fins, and snorkel. The best prices for gear, as you might imagine, are not to be found at seaside resorts.

Snorkeling gear can be rented for a small charge from nearly every hotel.

Surfing

The best surfing is available on the east coast, and most wave riders congregate at the Soup Bowl, near Bathsheba. An annual international surfing competition is held on Barbados every November.

Waterskiing

Some large hotels have their own waterskiing concessions, with special boats, equipment, and instructors. Many beaches in Barbados, however, are patrolled by private individuals who own boats and several sizes of skis; they will offer their services through a hotel or directly to vacationers, or can be hailed like taxis. Ask your hotel staff or other guests about their experiences with these entrepreneurs. Be *sure* they provide life vests and at least two people in the boat: one to drive and one to watch the skier at all times.

Waterskiing is widely available, often provided along St. James and Christ Church by the private speedboat owners. Inquire at your hotel, which can direct you to the nearest Sunfish sailing and Hobie Cat rentals as well.

Windsurfing

Windsurfing is as strenuous as it is exciting, so it may not be the sport to try on your first day out, unless you're already in excellent shape. As with most water sports, it is essential to windsurf with someone else around who can watch you and go for help if necessary.

Always wear a life vest and preferably a diveskin to protect your own skin from the sun. Avoid suntan oil that could make your feet slippery and interfere with your ability to stand on the board. Nike, Inc. makes athletic shoes specifically for water sports.

Windsurfing boards and equipment are often guest amenities at the larger hotels and can be rented by nonguests. The best place to learn and to practice is on the south coast at the **Barbados Windsurfing Club Hotel** (Maxwell, Christ Church Parish, tel. 809/428–9095).

Beaches

Barbados is blessed with some of the Caribbean's most beautiful beaches, all of them open to the public. (Access to hotel beaches may not always be public, but you can walk onto almost any beach from another one.)

West Coast Beaches

The west coast has the stunning coves and white-sand beaches that are dear to postcard publishers—plus calm, clear water for snorkeling, scuba diving, and swimming. The afternoon clouds and sunsets may seem to be right out of a Turner painting; because there is nothing but ocean between Barbados and Africa, the sunsets are rendered even more spectacular by the fine red sand that sometimes blows in from the Sahara.

While beaches here are seldom crowded, the west coast is not the place to find isolation. Owners of private boats stroll by, offering waterskiing, parasailing, and snorkel cruises. There are no concession stands per se, but hotels welcome nonguests for terrace lunches (wear a cover-up). Picnic items and necessities can be bought at the Sunset Crest shopping center in Holetown.

Beaches begin in the north at **Heywoods** (about a mile of sand) and continue almost unbroken to Bridgetown at **Brighton Beach,** a popular spot with locals. There is public access through the Barbados Beach Club and the Barbados Pizza House (both good for casual lunches), south of the Discovery Bay Hotel.

Good spots for swimming include **Paradise Beach,** just off the Cunard Paradise Village &

Beach Club; **Brandon's Beach,** a 10-minute walk south; **Browne's Beach,** in Bridgetown; and **Greaves End Beach,** south of Bridgetown at Aquatic Gap, between the Grand Barbados Beach Resort and the Hilton in St. Michael Parish.

The west coast is the area for scuba diving, sailing, and lunch-and-rum cruises on the red-sailed *Jolly Roger* "pirate" party ship (Fun Cruises, tel. 809/436–6424 or 809/429–4545). Somewhat more sedate sea experiences can be had on the *Wind Warrior* (tel. 809/425–5800) and the *Secret Love* (tel. 809/425–5800).

The *Atlantis* **submarine** (tel. 809/436–8929 or 809/436–8932) goes to depths of 150 feet off wrecks and reefs in a Canadian-built 50-foot submarine that seats 28 passengers at a time, each at his or her own porthole. Classical music plays while an oceanography specialist informs. *Cost: $69.50 per person.*

South Coast Beaches

The heavily traveled south coast of Christ Church Parish is much more built up than the St. James Parish coast in the west; here you'll find condos, high-rise hotels, many places to eat and shop, and the traffic (including public transportation) that serves them. These busier beaches generally draw a younger, more active crowd. The quality of the beach itself is consistently good, the reef-protected waters safe for swimming and snorkeling.

Needham's Point, with its lighthouse, is one of Barbados's best beaches, crowded with locals on weekends and holidays. Two others are in the St. Lawrence Gap area, near **Casuarina Cove.** The **Barbados Windsurfing Club Hotel** in Maxwell caters specifically to windsurfing aficionados, and most hotels and resorts provide boards or rent them for a nominal fee.

Crane Beach has for years been a popular swimming beach. As you move toward the Atlantic side of the island, the waves roll in bigger and faster; the waves at the nearby Crane Hotel are a favorite with bodysurfers. (But remember that this is the ocean, not the Caribbean, and exercise caution.)

Nearby **Foul Bay** lives up to its name only for sailboats; for swimmers and alfresco lunches, it's lovely.

North Coast Beaches

Those who love wild natural beauty will want to head north up the east-coast highway. With secluded beaches and crashing ocean waves on one side, rocky cliffs and verdant landscape on the other, the windward side of Barbados won't disappoint anyone who seeks dramatic views. But be cautioned: Swimming here is treacherous and *not* recommended. The waves are high, the bottom tends to be rocky, and the currents are unpredictable. Limit yourself to enjoying the view and watching the surfers—who have been at it since they were kids.

A worthwhile little-visited beach for the adventurous who don't mind trekking about a mile off the beaten track is **Morgan Lewis Beach,** on the coast east of Morgan Lewis Mill, the oldest intact windmill on the island. Turn east on the small road that goes to the town of Boscobelle (between Cherry Tree Hill and Morgan Lewis Mill), but instead of going to the town, take the even less traveled road (unmarked on most maps; you will have to ask for directions) that goes down the cliff to the beach. What awaits is more than 2 miles of unspoiled, uninhabited white sand and sweeping views of the Atlantic coastline. You may see a few Barbadians swimming, sunning, or fishing, but for the most part you'll have privacy.

Return to your car, cross the island's north point on the secondary roads until you reach the west coast. About a mile west from the end of Highway 1B is **Maycock's Bay,** an isolated area in St. Lucy Parish about 2 miles north of Heywoods, the west coast's northernmost resort complex.

6 Shopping

Shopping Districts

Traditionally, Broad Street and its side streets in Bridgetown have been the center for shopping action. Hours are generally weekdays 8–4, Saturday 8–1. Many stores have an in-bound (duty-free) department where you must show your travel tickets or a passport in order to buy duty-free goods.

Recently, several new areas opened their freshly painted doors. The mall-like **Sheraton Centre** (at Sargeant's Village in Christ Church) has toys for tots, togs for teens, and temptations for all. The **Quayside Shopping Center** (at Rockley in Christ Church) is smaller and more select, with frozen yogurt at **Toppings** and handmade articles at **Artworx** in Shop 5, where everything comes from Barbados, Trinidad, St. Lucia, or Guyana.

Best 'N The Bunch is both a wildly colored chattel house at The Chattel House Village (at St. Lawrence Gap) and its own best advertisement. Here the expert jewelry of Bajan David Trottman sells for that rarity—reasonable prices. **Perfections** also has good finds—all from Bajan artists—for men, women, and children, and **Beach Bum** offers teens "barely" bikinis.

Good Buys

Antiques   Antiques and fine memorabilia are the stock of **Greenwich House Antiques** (tel. 809/432–1169) in Greenwich Village, Trents Hill, St. James Parish, and at **Antiquaria** (tel. 809/426–0635) on St. Michael's Row next to the Anglican cathedral in Bridgetown.

Chic Shops   Hidden in separate corners of Barbados are some very upscale, little-known shops that can hold their own in New York or London. Carol Cadogan's **Cotton Days Designs** at Rose Cottage (Lower Bay St., tel. 809/427–7191) and on the Wharf in Bridgetown sets the international pace with all-cotton, collage creations that have been declared "wearable art." These are fantasy designs, with prices that begin at U.S.$250. Fortunately, she takes credit cards.

Corrie Scott, owner of **Corrie's** (Bay St. in Hastings, tel. 809/427–9184), designs hand-knit cotton sweaters and dresses that begin at U.S.$75; she also carries jewelry by David Trottman, as well as the exotic dress designs of Derek Went.

Another shop worth a visit on the Wharf is **Origins** (tel. 809/436–8522), where original hand-painted and dyed clothing, imported cottons, linens, and silks for day and evening, and hand-made jewelry and accessories are the order of the day. The hand-painted T-shirts are especially good here.

In St. Michael, stop in at **Petal's** in the Barbados Hilton shopping arcade for fashionable shoes and handbags: Friendly service and good-quality items make this shop special.

Handicrafts   Island handicrafts are everywhere: woven mats and place mats, dresses, dolls, handbags, shell jewelry. The **Best of Barbados** shops, at the Sandpiper Inn, Mall 34 in Bridgetown (tel. 800/436–1410), and three other locations, offer the highest-quality artwork and crafts, both "native style" and modern designs. A resident artist, Jill Walker, sells her watercolors and prints here and at **Walker's World** shops near the south shore hotels in St. Lawrence Gap.

At the **Pelican Village Handicrafts Center** on the Princess Alice Highway near the Cheapside Market in Bridgetown, in a cluster of conical shops, you can watch goods and crafts being made before you purchase them. Rugs and mats made from pandanus grass and khuskhus are good buys.

For native Caribbean arts and crafts, including items from Barbados and Haiti, try the Guard-house Gallery near the Grand Barbados Hotel in St. Michael. A selection of wooden, straw, and ceramic items is available.

Luxury Goods   Bridgetown stores have values on fine bone china, crystal, cameras, stereo and video equipment, jewelry, perfumes, and clothing. **Cave Shepherd** and **Harrison's** department stores offer wide selections of goods at many locations and at the airport. **De Lima's** and **Da Costa's Ltd.** stock high-quality imports. Among the specialty stores are **Louis I. Bayley** (gold watches),

J. Baldini (Brazilian jewelry and Danish silver), and **Correia's** (diamonds, pearls, semiprecious stones). The 20 small shops of **Mall 34** in Bridgetown's central district sell everything from luxury goods to crafts.

7 Dining

The better hotels and restaurants of Barbados have employed chefs trained in New York and Europe to attract and keep their sophisticated clientele. Gourmet dining here usually means fresh seafood, beef, or veal with finely blended sauces.

The native West Indian cuisine offers an entirely different dining experience. The island's West African heritage brought rice, peas, beans, and okra to its table, the staples that make a perfect base for slowly cooked meat and fish dishes. Many side dishes are cooked in oil (the pumpkin fritters can be addictive). And be cautious at first with the West Indian seasonings; like the sun, they are hotter than you think.

Every menu features dolphin (the fish, not the mammal), kingfish, snapper, and flying fish prepared every way imaginable. Shellfish abound; so does steak. Everywhere for breakfast and dessert you'll find mangoes, soursop, papaya (called pawpaw), and, in season, mammyapples, a basketball-size, thick-skinned fruit with giant seeds.

Cou-cou is a mix of cornmeal and okra with a spicy Creole sauce made from tomatoes, onions, and sweet peppers; steamed flying fish is often served over it. A version served by the Brown Sugar restaurant, called "red herring," is smoked herring and breadfruit in Creole sauce.

Pepperpot stew, a hearty mix of oxtail, beef chunks, and "any other meat you may have," simmered overnight, is flavored with *cassareep,* an ancient preservative and seasoning that gives the stew its dark, rich color.

Christophines and **eddoes** are tasty, potatolike vegetables that are often served with curried shrimp, chicken, or goat.

Buljol is a cold salad of codfish, tomatoes, onions, sweet peppers, and celery, marinated and served raw.

Callaloo is a soup made from okra, crabmeat, a spinachlike vegetable that gives the dish its name, and seasonings.

Among the liquid refreshments of Barbados, in addition to the omnipresent Banks Beer and

Mount Gay rum, there are **falernum**, a liqueur concocted of rum, sugar, lime juice, and almond essence, and **mauby**, a refreshing nonalcoholic beerlike drink made by boiling bitter bark and spices, straining the mixture, and sweetening it.

Barbados's British heritage and large resident population keep the island's dress code modest. While this does not always mean a tie and jacket, jeans, shorts, and beach shirts are frowned upon at dinnertime.

Highly recommended restaurants are indicated by a star ★.

Category	Cost*
Expensive	over $40
Moderate	$25–$40
Inexpensive	under $25

per person, excluding drinks and 5% service charge

Expensive

Bagatelle Great House. Occupying a converted plantation house in a hilly area, Bagatelle Great House gives diners an impression of colonial life. The terrace allows intimate dining at tables for two, while inside the castlelike walls there are much larger round tables. The superb ambience is somewhat more memorable than the expensive Continental dishes. *St. Thomas Parish, tel. 809/421–6767. Reservations necessary. Jacket and tie required. MC, V.*

★ **Carambola.** This romantic alfresco restaurant is set on a cliff overlooking the Caribbean in St. James Parish. Here, by candlelight, you can enjoy what is considered some of the best food in Barbados, created by British chef Paul Owens using traditional French recipes. Try the lobster or the more inventive dishes, such as the flying-fish salad and snapper with pimento sauce, or for dessert, the chocolate and lime pie. *Derricks, St. James Parish, tel. 809/432–0832. Reservations required. Dinner only. AE, MC, V.*

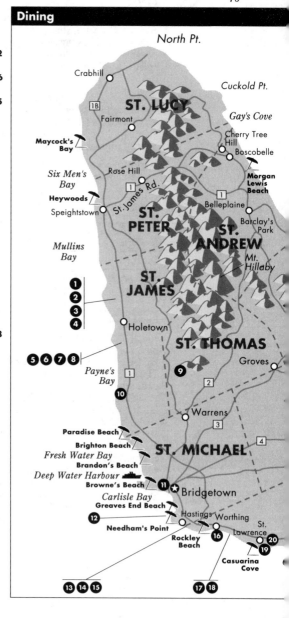

Dining

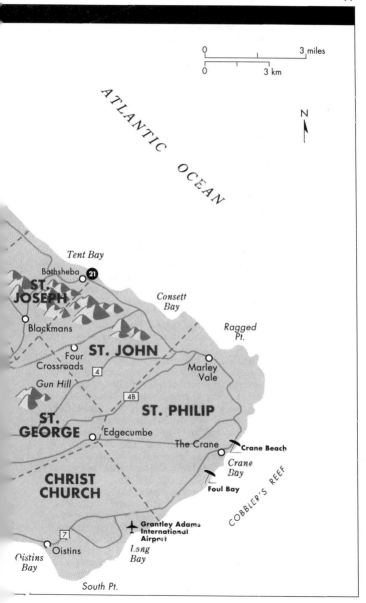

La Cage aux Folles. Acclaimed as one of the island's finest restaurants, La Cage aux Folles has moved to a new location, set in the restored Summerland Great House amid 2 acres of tropical gardens, and is lovelier than ever. The exotic five-course menu features international cuisine. Items include fresh fish with orange and Cointreau, sweet-and-sour shrimp, Malaysian satay, and sesame prawn pâté. *Prospect, St. James Parish, tel. 809/424–2424. Reservations necessary. Jacket and tie required. AE, MC, V. Dinner only. Closed Tues.*

The Palm Terrace. Arriving from London's Le Gavroche, the Palm's young British chef applies his talents to combine Barbadian produce with top-quality imports. The result is modern European creations, such as *mille feuille* of home-smoked chicken with tomato, chives, and carrots in a light mustard cream sauce for an appetizer. Home-grown mint accents New Zealand rack of lamb, and panfried crab becomes a stuffing for the breast of chicken entrée. Widely spaced tables, comfortable chairs, and indoor palms swaying under floor-to-ceiling arches create an ambience that is formal, yet relaxed as you dine facing the Caribbean Sea. *Royal Pavilion, Porters, St. James Parish, tel. 809/422–5555. Reservations advised. Dinner only. AE, DC, MC, V.*

★ **Raffles.** Young, international owners have made this one of Barbados's top restaurants. Forty guests can be seated at beautifully decorated tables featuring a tropical safari theme. Main dishes may be shrimp saki, blackened fish, steak served in a wine-and-lime sauce, basil-curry chicken, and sweet-and-sour pork. The desserts are both delicious and decadent. *1st St., Holetown, St. James Parish, tel. 809/432–6557 or 809/432–1280. Reservations necessary. Dinner only. AE, D, DC, MC, V.*

Sandy Bay Restaurant. Located at the renowned Sandy Lane Hotel, this is the perfect place for an elegant meal overlooking one of the best beaches on the island. The hotel's general manager brought British chef Mel Rumbles to the restaurant to create a menu that is both tasty and healthful. Grilled dolphin; lobster; and grilled lamb with honey, thyme, and wild rosemary are among the entrées. The vegetables, including local christophines and the delicate puréed pumpkin soup, are tasty. To ensure that the best produce is used, a van is sent out every morning to scour the island for the freshest vegetables and fish. The chef has also begun cultivating a spice and vegetable garden specifically to meet the hotel's needs. The desserts, created by a French pastry chef, are not to be missed, especially the dark chocolate truffle and the pecan pie with almond sauce. *Sandy Lane Hotel and Golf Club, St. James Parish, tel. 809/432–1311. AE, MC, V.*

Moderate

Brown Sugar. A special-occasion atmosphere prevails at Brown Sugar, located just behind the Island Inn outside Bridgetown. Dozens of ferns and hanging plants decorate the breezy multilevel restaurant. The extensive and authentic West Indian lunch buffets, served between 11:30 and 2:30 and popular with local businessmen, include cou-cou, pepperpot stew, Creole orange chicken, and such homemade desserts as angelfood chocolate mousse cake and passion fruit and nutmeg ice cream. *Aquatic Gap, St. Michael Parish, tel. 809/426-7684. Reservations recommended. AE, MC.*

★ **Fathoms.** Veteran restaurateurs Stephen and Sandra Toppin have opened their newest property seven days a week, for lunch and dinner, with 22 well-dressed tables scattered from the inside dining rooms to the patio's ocean edge. Dinner may bring a grilled lobster, island rabbit, jumbo baked shrimp, or cashew-crusted kingfish. This place is casual by day, candlelit by night. *Payne's Bay, St. James Parish, tel. 809/432-2568. Reservations advised for dinner. AE, MC, V.*

★ **Ile de France.** French owners Martine (from Lyon) and Michel (from Toulouse) Gramaglia have adapted the pool and garden areas of the Windsor Arms Hotel and turned them into an island "in" spot. White latticework opens to the night sounds; soft taped French music plays; and a single, perfect hibiscus dresses each table. Just a few of their specialties: foie gras; tournedos Rossini; lobster-and-crepe flambé; and filet Mignon with a choice of pepper, béarnaise, or champignon sauce. *Windsor Arms Hotel, Hastings, Christ Church Parish, tel. 809/435-6869. Reservations required. No credit cards. Dinner only. Closed Mon.*

Josef's. Swede Nils Ryman created a menu from the unusual combination of Caribbean cooking—blackened fish in which the fish is fried, rolled in Cajun spices, and seared in oil before being slightly baked in the oven—and Scandinavian fare—Toast Skagen made from diced shrimp blended with mayonnaise and fresh dill. Stroll around the garden before moving to the alfresco dining room downstairs or to the simply decorated room upstairs for a table that looks out over the sea. *Waverly House, St. Lawrence Gap, tel. 809/435-6541. Reservations advised. AE, DC, MC, V.*

La Maison. The elegant, colonial-style Balmore House reopened in October 1990 under the ownership of Geoffrey Farmer. The atmosphere is created by English country furnishings and a paneled bar opening onto a seaside terrace for dining. A French chef from the Loire Valley creates seafood specials, including a flying-fish parfait appetizer. Passion-fruit ice cream highlights the dessert menu. Lunch and dinner. *Holetown, St. James Parish, tel. 809/432-1156. Reservations recommended. D, MC, V.*

★ **Ocean View Hotel.** This elegant pink grande dame hotel is dressed in fresh fabrics, with great bunches of equally fresh flowers and sparkling crystal chandeliers. Bajan dishes are featured for lunch and dinner, and the Sunday-only Planter's Luncheon Buffet in the downstairs Club Xanadu (which fronts the beach) offers course after course of traditional dishes. Pianist Jean Emerson plays Hoagy Carmichael tunes and sings in dusky tones. *Hastings, Christ Church Parish, tel. 809/427-7821. Reservations recommended. AE, MC, V.*

Pisces. For Caribbean seafood at the water's edge, this restaurant in lively St. Lawrence Gap specializes in seasonal dishes. Fish is the way to go here—flying fish, dolphin, crab, kingfish, shrimp, prawns, and lobster—prepared any way from charbroiled to sautéed. There are also some chicken and beef dishes. Other items include conch fritters, tropical gazpacho, and seafood terrine with a mango sauce. Enjoy a meal in a contemporary setting filled with hanging tropical plants. *St. Lawrence Gap, Christ Church Parish, tel. 809/435-6564. Reservations recommended. Dinner only during low season. AE, MC, V.*

Plantation. Wednesday's Bajan buffet and Tuesday's entertainment are big attractions here. The Plantation is set in a renovated Barbadian residence surrounded by spacious grounds above the Southwinds Resort; its cuisine combines French and Barbadian influences, and you can eat indoors or on the terrace. *St. Lawrence, Christ Church Parish, tel. 809/428-5048. Reservations suggested. AE, MC, V. Dinner only.*

Rose and Crown. The casual Rose and Crown serves a variety of fresh seafood, but it's the local lobster that's high on diners' lists. Indoors is a paneled bar, outdoors are tables on a wraparound porch. *Prospect, St. James Parish, tel. 809/425-1074. Reservations suggested. AE, MC, V. Dinner served 6-10.*

The Virginian. The locally popular Virginian offers intimate surroundings and some of the island's best dining values. The specialties are seafood, shrimp, and steaks. *Sea View Hotel, Hastings, Christ Church Parish, tel. 809/427-7963, ext. 121. Reservations suggested. AE, MC, V. Dinner only.*

Witch Doctor. The interior of the Witch Doctor is decorated with pseudo-African art that gives a lighthearted carefree atmosphere to this casual hangout across the street from the sea; the menu features traditional Barbadian dishes, European fare, and local seafood. *St. Lawrence Gap, Christ Church Parish, tel. 809/435-6581. Reservations recommended. MC, V. Dinner only.*

Inexpensive

Atlantis Hotel. While the surroundings may be simple and the rest room could use a coat of paint, the nonstop food and the magnificent ocean view at the Atlantis Hotel in Bathsheba make it a real find. Owner-chef Enid Maxwell serves up an enormous Bajan buffet daily, where you're likely to find pickled souse (marinated pig parts and vegetables), pumpkin fritters, spinach balls, pickled breadfruit, fried "fline" (flying) fish, roast chicken, pepperpot stew, and West Indian–style okra and eggplant. Among the homemade pies are an apple and a dense coconut. *Bathsheba, St. Joseph Parish, tel. 809/433–9445. Reservations suggested. No credit cards.*

★ **David's Place.** Here you'll be served first-rate dishes in a first-rate location—a black-and-white Bajan cottage overlooking St. Lawrence Bay. Specialties include Baxters Road chicken, local flying fish, pepperpot (salt pork, beef, and chicken boiled and bubbling in a spicy cassareep stock), and curried shrimp. Homemade cheesebread is served with all dishes. Desserts might be banana pudding, coconut-cream pie, carrot cake with rum sauce, or cassava pone. *St. Lawrence Main Road, Worthing, Christ Church Parish, tel. 809/435–6550. Reservations preferred. AE, MC, V.*

Nico's. This small second-floor bistro is a cheery, intimate gathering spot for ex-patriates and visitors. An oval bar, surrounded by stools, stands in the middle of the room, with the tables on the perimeter and a few more on the terrace above the street. Come to Nico's for drinks and to socialize, as well as order off the blackboard menu something small, like deep-fried Camembert, or more substantial, such as seafood thermidor. *Second St., Holetown, tel. 809/432–6386. MC, V.*

The Waterfront Cafe. Located on the Careenage, a sliver of sea in Bridgetown, this is the perfect place to enjoy a drink, snack, or meal. Locals and tourists gather here for sandwiches, salads, fish, steak-and-kidney pie, and casseroles. The panfried flying-fish sandwich is especially tasty. From the brick-and-mirrored interior you can gaze through the arched windows, enjoy the cool trade winds and let time pass. *Bridgetown, St. Michael Parish, tel. 809/427–0093. MC, V. Dress: casual. Live jazz Mon.–Sat. Food served 10–10, open until midnight.*

8 Lodging

The southern and western shores of Barbados are lined with hotels and resorts of every size and price, offering a variety of accommodations from private villas to modest but comfortable rooms in simple inns. At the same time, apartment and home rentals and time-share condominiums have become widely available and are growing increasingly popular among visitors to the island. A few of Barbados's hotels have recently become all-inclusive, though most still offer either EP or MAP meal plans.

Choosing the location of your hotel is important. Hotels to the north of Bridgetown, in the parishes of St. Peter, St. James, and St. Michael, tend to be more self-contained resorts with stretches of empty road between them that discourage strolling to a neighborhood bar or restaurant. Southwest of Bridgetown, in Christ Church Parish, many of the hotels cluster near or along the busy strip known as St. Lawrence Gap, where small restaurants, bars, and nightclubs are close by.

Hotels listed are grouped here by parish, beginning with St. James in the west and St. Peter to the north, then St. Michael, Christ Church, St. Philip, and St. Joseph.

Highly recommended lodgings are indicated by a star ★.

Category	Cost*
Very Expensive	over $350
Expensive	$250–$350
Moderate	$150–$250
Inexpensive	under $150

All prices are for a standard double room, excluding 5% government tax and 10% service charge.

St. James Parish

Coral Reef Club. Days here are spent relaxing on the white-sand beach or around the pool, with time taken out for the hotel's superb afternoon tea. The public areas ramble along the beach and face the Caribbean Sea, with small coralstone cottages scattered over the surrounding 12 flower-filled acres. (The cottages farthest from the beach are a bit of a hike to the main house.) The accommodations are spacious, each with air-conditioning and ceiling fans, a small patio terrace, and fresh flowers. The restaurant, under the direction of Bajan chef, Graham Licorish, is noted for its inventive cuisine that combines local cooking with European flair. Most guests are on a MAP plan that includes a complimentary buffet lunch. Another convenience is the free shuttle into Bridgetown. *Porters, St. James Parish, tel. 809/422–2372, fax 809/422–1776. 70 rooms. Facilities: pool, entertainment. AE, MC, V. EP. Very Expensive.*

★ **Glitter Bay.** In the 1930s, Sir Edward Cunard, of the English shipping family, bought this estate, built the main Great House and a beach house similar to his palazzo in Venice, and began hosting famous parties in honor of visiting aristocrats and celebrities, making Glitter Bay synonomous with grandeur. Today, new buildings, angled back from the beach, house 81 one- to three-bedroom suites (each with a full kitchen) that have recently been refurbished, and the beach house has been transformed into five garden suites. Manicured landscaped gardens separate the reception area and the large, comfortable tea lounge from the pool, the alfresco dining room where evening entertainment is held, and the half mile of crunchy beach. Glitter Bay is more casual and family oriented than its next-door sister property, the Royal Pavilion, but they share facilities, including complimentary water sports and dining privileges at either resort. *Porters, St. James Parish, tel. 809/422–4111, fax 809/422–3940. 86 rooms. Facilities: pool, restaurant, water sports, 2 lighted tennis courts, golf course nearby. AE, DC, MC, V. EP, MAP. Very Expensive.*

★ **The Royal Pavilion.** Seventy-two of the 75 rooms here are oceanfront suites; the remaining three are nestled in a garden villa. The ground-floor oceanfront rooms allow guests simply to step through sliding doors, cross their private patio, and walk onto the sands. Second- and third-floor rooms, however, have the advantage of an ele-

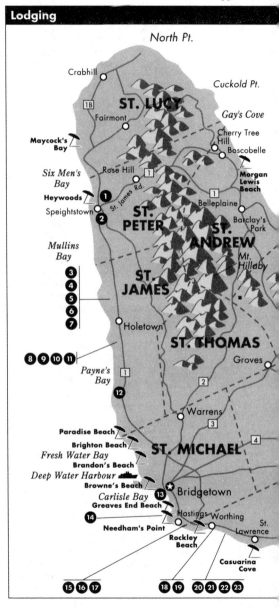

Lodging

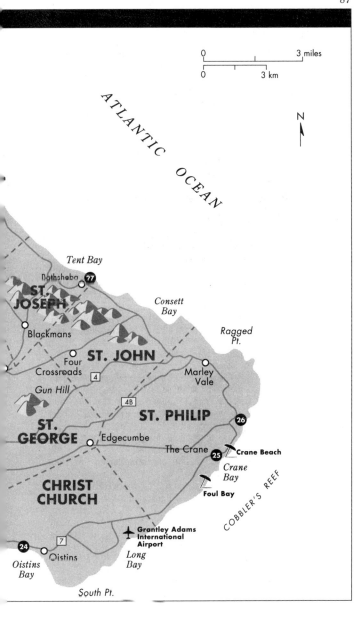

vated view of the sea. Breakfast and lunch are served alfresco along the edge of the beach. Afternoon tea and dinner are in the Palm Terrace (*see* Dining in Chapter 7). The Royal Pavilion attracts the sophisticated guest who wants serenity (children under 12 are discouraged during the winter months), but are welcome to share the facilities of its adjoining sister hotel, the more informal Glitter Bay. *Porters, St. James Parish, tel. 809/422–5555, fax 809/422–3940. 75 rooms. Facilities: 2 restaurants, 2 bars, 2 lighted, artificial-grass tennis courts, supperclub entertainment, water-sports center, golf course nearby. AE, D, DC, MC, V. EP. Very Expensive.*

★ **Sandy Lane Hotel.** The complete renovation of this prestigious hotel has given it good reason to remain the island's most expensive property. If you like low-key luxury set on one of the best beaches in Barbados, Sandy Lane is the place. One choice room is 310, with a large private balcony for breakfast and for watching magnificent sunsets in the evening. It has a huge king-size bed and a vast bathroom, complete with double washbasin, a deep oval tub, and bidet. Afternoon tea, fine dining, and personalized service all add to the charm. The white coral structure, finished with Zandobbio marble throughout and a staircase leading to the beach shaded with mahogany trees, is reminiscent of *The Great Gatsby. Hwy. 1, St. James Parish, tel. 809/432–1311, fax 809/432–2954. 91 doubles, 30 suites. Facilities: free water sports, 18-hole golf course and club, pool, 5 tennis courts (2 floodlit); two oceanfront restaurants, poolside snack bar, 5 bars, live entertainment nightly. AE, DC, MC, V. EP, MAP. Very Expensive.*

Settlers' Beach. The accommodations at Settlers' Beach are two-story, two-bedroom homes with full kitchen and dining room (or one-story villas with atrium), arranged asymmetrically around a large courtyard filled with towering palms and a pool. The property is small, squeezed between newer resorts, and attracts those seeking a quiet vacation. *Hwy. 1, St. James Parish, tel. 809/422–3052, fax 809/422–1937. 22 villas. Facilities: pool, restaurant. AE, MC, V. EP. Very Expensive.*

Coconut Creek Club. A luxury cottage colony,

the Coconut Creek Club is set on handsomely landscaped grounds with a small but adequate private beach and a bar pavilion for entertainment and dancing. The atmosphere here is more casual than its sister hotel, the Colony Club. *Reservations: Box 249, Bridgetown; Hwy. 1, St. James Parish, tel. 809/432–0803, fax 809/422–1726. 53 rooms. Facilities: pool, dining room, pub. AE, DC, MC, V, EP, MAP. Expensive.*

Discovery Bay Hotel. The rooms of the quiet, white-columned, recently renovated Discovery Bay Hotel open onto a central lawn and a pool. Some rooms have ocean views. *Hwy. 1, Holetown, St. James Parish, tel. 809/432–1301, fax 809/422–1726. 85 rooms. Facilities: pool, table tennis, terrace restaurant, boutique, water sports. AE, MC, V. EP. Expensive.*

Treasure Beach. Under a new manageress, this compact resort, with small one-bedroom suites, is tightly run. The ground-floor rooms offer little privacy from other guests unless the shutters are closed, so you may wish to be on the second or third floor. Most of the rooms overlook the small garden, a few have sea views. The atmosphere is casual, and the staff is equally so. *Payne's Bay, St. James Parish, tel. 809/432–1346, fax 809/432–1740. 24 one-bedroom, air-conditioned suites; 1 two-bedroom penthouse suite. Facilities: restaurant, pool, water sports. AE, DC, MC, V. EP, MAP. Expensive.*

Almond Beach Club. In this hotel, everything is included in the price of the room—all you want to eat and drink (that includes wine and liquor); water sports; boat trips; tennis; tours of the island; shopping excursions to Bridgetown; accommodations, mostly in one-bedroom suites with balconies; departure transportation to the airport; and service and taxes. The food is excellent, from the breakfast buffet and a four-course lunch to the afternoon tea and pastries and the extensive dinner menu. Menus offer plenty of choice, but if your stay is seven days or more and you want something different, Almond Beach Club offers a dine-around program—dinner or lunch at a number of area restaurants with round-trip transportation included. The Almond Beach Club has none of the enforced-activity, "whistle-blowing" atmosphere of some all-inclusives. *Vauxhall, St. James, tel. 809/*

432–7840 or 800/966–4737, fax 407/994–6344. 147 rooms. Facilities: restaurant, 3 pools, snorkeling, fishing, windsurfing, waterskiing, tennis, squash, sauna, fitness center. AE, MC, V. All-inclusive. Moderate–Expensive.

Barbados Beach Village. Vacationers choose from twin-bedded rooms, studios, apartments, and duplexes at the Barbados Beach Village. The beach has a terrace bar, and the restaurant is seaside. *Hwy. 1, St. James Parish, tel. 809/425–1440, fax 809/424–0996. 88 rooms. Facilities: pool, restaurant, disco nightclub. AE, DC, MC, V. EP. Moderate.*

St. Peter Parish

★ **Cobblers Cove Hotel.** This all-suite hotel, renovated in 1992, 12 miles up the west coast from Bridgetown, combines comfort and informal elegance. Each luxury suite has a balcony or patio and wet bar. The pink-and-white buildings contrasting with tropical gardens overlooking the sea create a fine retreat that recently joined the Relais et Château marketing group. The atmosphere is casual and smart, with a clublike lounge-library and a bar that becomes the evening gathering spot. *Hwy. 1, St. Peter Parish, tel. 809/422–2291, fax 809/422–1460. 38 suites plus the Camelot Suite, with king-size, four-poster bed; whirlpool bath; private pool; and lounge. Facilities: pool, floodlit tennis court, water sports, child care available, but no children under 12 allowed at hotel late Jan.–late March. Closed Sept. AE, MC, V. CP, MAP. Very Expensive.*

Heywoods Barbados. Everything is on a grand scale here: The seven buildings of the Heywoods Barbados, each with its own theme and decor, house hundreds of rooms. The mile-long beach has space for all water sports. Now a Wyndham resort, the property is well laid out to accept large groups. *Hwy. 1, St. Peter Parish, tel. 809/422–4900, fax 809/422–1581. 306 rooms. Facilities: 3 pools, 5 lighted tennis courts, squash courts, 9-hole golf course, restaurants, bars, boutiques, entertainment. AE, DC, MC, V. All-inclusive. Moderate.*

St. Michael Parish

Grand Barbados Beach Resort. A mile from Bridgetown on Carlisle Bay, this convenient hotel has pleasant rooms and suites. The white-sand beach is lapped by a surprisingly clear sea, despite the oil refinery close by. The Aquatic Club executive floor has rooms that include a Continental breakfast and secretarial services suitable for business travelers. A 260-foot-long pier for romantic walks, plus live music and a dance floor, enhance a stay here. *Box 639, Bridgetown, St. Michael Parish, tel. 809/426–0890 or 800/223–9815, fax 809/424–0096. 133 rooms. Facilities: beach, pool, exercise room, whirlpool, sauna, shopping arcade, beauty salon/barber shop, 2 restaurants. AE, DC, MC, V. EP. Expensive.*

Barbados Hilton International. This large resort, just five minutes from Bridgetown, is for those who like activity and having plenty of people around. Expect to rub shoulders with delegates attending seminars and conventioneers, and don't be surprised by the strong odor from the nearby oil refinery. Its attractions include an atrium lobby, a man-made beach 1,000 feet wide with full water sports, and lots of shops. All rooms and suites have balconies. *Needham's Point, St. Michael Parish, tel. 809/426–0200, fax 809/436–8646. 185 rooms. Facilities: pool, tennis courts, restaurant, lounge, health club. AE, DC, MC, V. EP. Moderate–Expensive.*

Christ Church Parish

Divi Southwinds Beach Resort. In this resort, situated on 20 lush acres, the toss-up is whether to take one of the one-bedroom suites, with a balcony and kitchenette overlooking the gardens and pool, or one of the smaller and older-looking rooms, just steps from the white sandy beach. Though all the rooms are pleasant, the buildings themselves have a barracks ambience. Dining facilities next to the pool have the tour-package feel, with the emphasis on self-service. Guests come here for a rollicking good time that includes making full use of the scuba and water-sports facilities. *St. Lawrence, Christ Church Parish, tel. 800/367–3484, fax 809/428–4674. 166 rooms. Facilities: 2 restaurants, 3 pools, 2* *lighted tennis courts, putting green, shopping arcade. AE, DC, MC, V. EP, MAP. Expensive.*

Southern Palms. A plantation-style hotel on a 1,000-foot stretch of pink sand near the Dover Convention Center, Southern Palms is a convenient businessperson's hotel. You may choose from standard bedrooms, deluxe oceanfront suites with kitchenettes, and a four-bedroom penthouse. Each wing of the hotel has its own small pool. *St. Lawrence, Christ Church Parish, tel. 809/428-7171, fax 809/428-7175. 93 rooms. Facilities: 2 pools, duty-free shop, small conference center, miniature-golf course, tennis court, dining room, water sports. AE, D, DC, MC, V. EP. Expensive.*

Casuarina Beach Club. This luxury apartment hotel on 900 feet of pink sand takes its name from the casuarina pines that surround it, and the quiet setting provides a dramatic contrast to that of the platinum-coast resorts. The bar and restaurant are on the beach. A new reception area includes small lounges where guests can get a dose of TV—there aren't any in the bedrooms. Scuba diving, golf, and other activities can be arranged. The Casuarina Beach is popular with those who prefer self-catering holidays in a secluded setting, convenient to nightlife and shopping. *St. Lawrence Gap, Christ Church Parish, tel. 809/428-3600, fax 809/428-1970. 134 rooms. Facilities: pool, tennis courts, squash courts, restaurant, bar, minimarket, duty-free shop. AE, MC, V. EP. Moderate.*

Club Rockley Barbados. At press time, part of these time-share condominiums was being transformed into an all-inclusive resort with air-conditioned one- and two-bedroom accommodations, with a balcony or a patio. On the grounds are a massage center; six swimming pools; five tennis courts; a 9-hole golf course; squash courts; a free shuttle bus to the beach (five minutes); two dining rooms, one offering buffet dinners and another with an à la carte menu; a disco for late-night revelry; and a children's program. *Christ Church Parish, tel. 809/435-7880, fax 809/435-8015. 288 rooms. AE, DC, MC, V. All-inclusive. Moderate.*

Sandy Beach Hotel. On a wide, sparkling white beach, this comfortable hotel has a popular poolside bar and the Green House Restaurant, which serves a weekly West Indian buffet. All rooms have kitchenettes. Water sports, at extra cost, include scuba-diving certification, deep-sea fishing, harbor cruises, catamaran sailing, and windsurfing. Guests can walk to St. Lawrence Gap for other restaurants and entertainment. *Worthing, Christ Church Parish, tel. 809/435–8000, fax 809/435–8053. 89 units. Facilities: pool, restaurant, bar, entertainment. AE, D, DC, MC, V. EP. Moderate.*

Accra Beach Hotel. A complete renovation of the rooms should inject new life into this utilitarian hotel on the beach. The rooms obliquely face a small lawn area, permitting an angled view of the sea. Dining on the other side of the garden adjacent to the pool provides the focus for guests. *Rockley Beach, Christ Church Parish, tel. 809/427–7866 or 800/223–9815, fax 809/435–6794. 52 rooms. Facilities: dining room, lounge, beach bar, water-sports center. AE, MC, V. EP. Inexpensive.*

Benston Windsurfing Club Hotel. A small hotel that began as a gathering place for windsurfing enthusiasts, the Benston Windsurfing Club is now a complete school and center for the sport. The rooms are spacious and sparsely furnished to accommodate the active and young crowd who choose this bare-bones hotel right on the beach. The bar and restaurant overlook the water. All sports can be arranged, but windsurfing (learning, practicing, and perfecting it) is king. *Maxwell Main Rd., Christ Church Parish, tel. 809/428–9095, fax 809/435–6621. 15 rooms. Facilities: restaurant, bar, entertainment. AE, MC, V. EP. Inexpensive.*

Little Bay Hotel. This small hotel is a find for anyone who wants to go easy on the wallet and yet sleep to the sounds of the sea. Each room has a private balcony, bedroom, small lounge, and kitchenette. Room 100 is a favorite. This year the owner, Charlene Paterson from Toronto, planned to throw away the drab carpets and replace them with a clay-tile floor. There are no TVs in the rooms, but guests can catch up on the news and watch sports in the small lounge next to the popular restaurant, Southern Accents. *St. Lawrence Gap, tel. 809/435–8574, fax 809/435–8586. 10 rooms. Facilities: lounge, bar, restaurant. AE, MC, V. EP. Inexpensive.*

★ **Ocean View.** Possibly the best-kept secret in the Caribbean, the 40 rooms and suites of this individualistic hideaway are home to celebrities on their commute to private villas in Mustique. The rooms vary considerably, and their charm depends on whether you appreciate the eclectic furnishings. Although it lacks modern amenities, bear in mind that this is an old colonial-style building and enjoy it for that. Owner John Chandler places his personal antiques throughout his three-story grande dame nestled against the sea, adds great bouquets of tropical flowers everywhere, and calls it home. In season, the downstairs Xanadu Club presents very good, off-off-Broadway reviews. *Hastings, Christ Church Parish, tel. 809/427–7821, fax 809/427–7826. 40 rooms. Facilities: restaurant and bar, supper club. AE, MC, V. CP. Inexpensive.*

Sichris Hotel. The Sichris is a "discovery," more attractive inside than seen from the road, a comfortable and convenient self-contained resort that can be ideal for businesspeople who need a quiet place in which to work. Just minutes from the city, the air-conditioned one-bedroom suites all have kitchenettes and private balconies or patios. It's a walk of two or three minutes to the beach. *Worthing, Christ Church Parish, tel. 809/435–7930, fax 809/435–8232. 24 rooms. Facilities: pool, restaurant, bar. AE, MC, V. EP. Inexpensive.*

St. Philip Parish

★ **Crane Beach Hotel.** This remote hilltop property on a cliff overlooking the dramatic Atlantic coast remains one of the special places of Barbados. The Crane Beach has suites and one-bedroom apartments in the main building. Room rates vary considerably. Corner suite 1 is one of the nicest, with its two walls of windows and patio terrace. The Roman-style pool with columns separates the main house from the dining room. To reach the beach, you walk down some 200 steps onto a beautiful stretch of sand thumped by waves that are good both for body surfing and swimming. *Crane Bay, St. Philip Parish, tel. 809/423–6220, fax 809/423–5343. 18 rooms. Facilities: pool, restaurant, 2 bars. AE, DC, MC, V. EP, MAP. Expensive.*

Marriott's Sam Lord's Castle. Set on the Atlantic coast about 14 miles east of Bridgetown, Sam Lord's Castle is not a castle with moat and towers but a sprawling great house surrounded by 72 acres of grounds, gardens, and beach. The seven rooms in the main house have canopied beds; downstairs, the public rooms have furniture by Sheraton, Hepplewhite, and Chippendale—unfortunately, for admiring, not for sitting. Additional guest rooms in surrounding cottages have more-conventional hotel furnishings. The beach is a mile long, the Wanderer Restaurant offers Continental cuisine, and there are even a few slot machines, as befits a pirate's lair. *Long Bay, St. Philip Parish, tel. 809/423-7350, fax 809/423-5918. 256 rooms. Facilities: 3 pools, lighted tennis courts, 3 restaurants, entertainment. AE, DC, MC, V. EP, MAP. Moderate.*

St. Joseph Parish

Atlantis Hotel. The Atlantis provides a warm, pleasant atmosphere in a pastoral location overlooking a majestically rocky Atlantic coast. The hotel is modest, yet the congeniality and the Bajan food more than make up for that. *Bathsheba, St. Joseph Parish, tel. 809/433-9445. 16 rooms. Facilities: dining room. AE. EP. Inexpensive.*

Rental Homes and Apartments

Private homes are available for rent south of Bridgetown in the Hastings–Worthing area, along the St. James Parish coast, and in St. Peter Parish. The **Barbados Board of Tourism** (tel. 809/427-2623) has a listing of rental properties and prices.

Villas and private home rentals are also available through Barbados realtors. Among them are **Alleyne, Aguilar & Altman,** Rosebank, St. James (tel. 809/432-0840); **Bajan Services,** St. Peter (tel. 809/422-2618); **Ronald Stoute & Sons Ltd.,** St. Philip (tel. 809/423-6800).

In the United States, contact **At Home Abroad** (tel. 212/421-9165) or Jan Pizzi at **Villa Vacations** (tel. 617/593-8885 or 800/800-5576).

9 The Arts and Nightlife

The Arts

Barbados Art Council. The gallery shows drawings, paintings, and other art, with a new show about every two weeks. *2 Pelican Village, Bridgetown, tel. 809/426–4385. Admission free. Open Mon.–Fri. 10–5, Sat. 9–1.*

A selection of private art galleries offers Bajan and West Indian art at collectible prices. **The Studio Art Gallery** (Fairchild St., Bridgetown, tel. 809/427–5463) exhibits local work (particularly that of Rachael Altman) and will frame purchases. The **Queen's Park Gallery** (Queen's Park, Bridgetown, tel. 809/427–2345) is run by the National Culture Foundation and is the island's largest gallery, presenting month-long exhibits. **Artworx** (Shop 5, Quayside Centre, Christ Church Parish, tel. 809/435–8112) is the most recent entry, selling only handmade items, from carved wooden trains, pottery, and ceramic jewelry to watercolors and prints.

Nightlife

When the sun goes down, the musicians come out, and folks go limin' in Barbados (anything from hanging out to a chat-up or jump-up). Competitions among reggae groups, steel bands, and calypso singers are major events, and tickets can be hard to come by, but give it a try.

Most of the large resorts have weekend shows aimed at visitors, and there is a selection of dinner shows that are a Barbados-only occasion. The cultural, folklore dinner show **1627 And All That** is held at the Barbados Museum on Thursday and Sunday. There's transportation to and from your hotel, hot hors d'oeuvres, a buffet dinner (with a l-o-n-g line), an open bar, and a good show put on by the Barbados Dance Theatre that combines history and folklore with calypso, limbo, and stilt dancing. *Hwy. 7, Garrison Savannah, tel. 809/435–6900. $41. Reservations recommended. AE, MC, V. Show and dinner, Sun. and Thurs.*

If it's Monday, it must be the **Plantation Tropical Spectacular** at the Plantation and Garden Theatre, with the internationally known Merrymen making the music and dance. It's a high-energy calypso show with fire-eaters, flaming limbo dancers, steel bands, and calypso, preceded by dinner and drinks, for $42 (show and drinks only, $17.50). Wednesday and Friday, the contemporary group Barbados By Night with Spice performs, and Saturday is a complete musical show. *St. Lawrence Rd., Christ Church Parish, tel. 809/428–5048. Reservations recommended. AE, DC, MC, V.*

The **Xanadu** is a mid-December through April cabaret, and on Thursday and Friday nights, that's the hottest ticket in town. David McCarty, who danced on Broadway and with the New York City Ballet, has joined forces with chanteuse Jean Emerson, and, along with local strutters, they put on the best show in town. Dinner in the upstairs flower-decked dining room is $44 for dinner and show; cabaret admission only, approximately $12.50. *Ocean View Hotel, Hastings, tel. 809/427–7821. Reservations required.*

Island residents have their own favorite night spots that change with the seasons. The most popular one is still **After Dark** (St. Lawrence Gap, Christ Church, tel. 809/435–6547), with the longest bar on the island and a jazz-club annex.

Harbour Lights claims to be the "home of the party animal," and most any night features live music with dancing under the stars. *On the Bay, Marine Villa, Bay St., St. Michael, tel. 809/ 436–7225.*

Another "in" spot, **Front Line** (Wharf St., tel. 809/429–6160) at the Wharf in Bridgetown, attracts a young crowd for its Reggae music.

Disco moves are made on the floor at the **Hippo Disco** in the Barbados Beach Village Hotel (St. James, tel. 809/425–1440), and above it, where dancers gyrate until the early hours of the morning.

Another dusky disco, **Club Miliki** (tel. 809/422–4900), takes center stage at the Heywoods Resort in St. Peter. Live music begins at 9 PM Friday and Saturday.

A late-night (after 11) excursion to **Baxter Road** is de rigueur for midnight Bajan street snacks, local rum, great gossip, and good lie telling. **Enid & Livy's** and **Collins** are just two of the many long-standing favorites. The later, the better.

Bars and Inns   Barbados supports the rum industry in more than 1,600 "rum shops," simple bars where men congregate to discuss the world's ills, and in more sophisticated inns, where you'll find world-class rum drinks and the island's renowned Mount Gay and Cockspur rums. The following offer welcoming spirits: **The Ship Inn** (St. Lawrence Gap, Christ Church Parish, tel. 809/435–6961), **The Coach House** (Paynes Bay, St. James Parish, tel. 809/432–1163), and **Harry's Oasis** (St. Lawrence, Christ Church Parish, no phone); **Bert's Bar** at the Abbeville Hotel (Rockley, Christ Church Parish, tel. 809/435–7924) serves the best daiquiris in town . . . any town. Also try **The Boat Yard** (Bay Street, Bridgetown, tel. 809/436–2622), **The Waterfront Cafe** (Bridgetown, tel. 809/427–0093), **The Warehouse** (Bridgetown, tel. 809/436–2897), and **TGI Boomers** (St. Lawrence Gap, Christ Church Parish, tel. 809/428–8439).

Barbados Hotels

	Accepts credit cards	Good Value	Luxurious	Secluded	All-inclusive	Good for families	Children's programs	Access for disabled	
Accra Beach Hotel	•								
Almond Beach Club	•	•	•		•	•	•	•	
Atlantis Hotel	•	•							
Barbados Beach Village	•					•			
Barbados Hilton International	•		•						
Bension Windsurfing Club Hotel	•								
Casuarina Beach Club	•	•	•			•			
Club Rockley Barbados	•				•	•			
Cobblers Cove Hotel	•		•	•					
Coconut Creek Club	•		•						
Coral Reef Club	•		•					•	
Crane Beach Hotel	•		•	•		•			
Discovery Bay Hotel	•		•					•	
Divi Southwinds Beach Resort	•								
Glitter Bay	•		•	•		•		•	
Grand Barbados Beach Resort	•		•			•	•	•	
Heywoods Barbados	•		•		•	•	•	•	
Little Bay Hotel	•	•				•			
Marriott's Sam Lord's Castle	•		•			•	•		
Ocean View	•	•	•						
The Royal Pavilion	•		•			•		•	
Sandy Beach Hotel	•					•		•	
Sandy Lane Hotel	•		•			•	•		
Settlers' Beach	•					•			
Sichris Hotel	•					•		•	
Southern Palms	•					•			
Treasure Beach	•							•	

Restaurants	Swimming pools	On the beach	On-site water sports	Fitness facilities	Spa facilities	Tennis courts	Golf nearby	Air-conditioning	Direct-dial phones	Cable TV
1	1	•					•	•		•
2	3	•	•	•	•	1	•	•		•
1		•								
1	1	•	•			2	•	•		
1	1	•		•	•	4	•	•		•
1		•	•							
1	2	•		•		2		•	•	
3	6			•	•	5	•	•	•	
1	1	•	•			1	•	•	•	
1	1	•	•				•	•	•	
1	1	•	•			2	•	•		
1	1	•				4	•		•	
2	1	•				2	•	•	•	
1	2	•	•			2	•	•		•
1	2	•	•	•		4	•	•	•	
2	1	•	•	•			•	•	•	•
4	3	•	•			5	•	•	•	
1		•					•			
3	3			•		7		•	•	
1		•					•		•	
2	1	•	•	•		4	•	•	•	
1	1	•	•				•	•	•	•
2	1	•	•	•		5	•	•	•	•
1	1	•				2	•	•	•	
1	1						•	•	•	
1	2	•	•			2	•	•		
1	1	•					•	•	•	

Index

Personal Itinerary

Departure *Date*

Time

Transportation

Arrival *Date*   *Time*

Departure *Date*   *Time*

Transportation

Arrival *Date*   *Time*

Departure *Date*   *Time*

Transportation

Arrival *Date*   *Time*

Departure *Date*   *Time*

Transportation

Personal Itinerary

Arrival   *Date*   *Time*

Departure   *Date*   *Time*

Transportation

Arrival   *Date*   *Time*

Departure   *Date*   *Time*

Transportation

Arrival   *Date*   *Time*

Departure   *Date*   *Time*

Transportation

Arrival   *Date*   *Time*

Departure   *Date*   *Time*

Transportation

Personal Itinerary

Arrival   *Date*   *Time*

Departure   *Date*   *Time*

Transportation

Arrival   *Date*   *Time*

Departure   *Date*   *Time*

Transportation

Arrival   *Date*   *Time*

Departure   *Date*   *Time*

Transportation

Arrival   *Date*   *Time*

Departure   *Date*   *Time*

Transportation

Addresses

Name	*Name*
Address	*Address*
Telephone	*Telephone*
Name	*Name*
Address	*Address*
Telephone	*Telephone*
Name	*Name*
Address	*Address*
Telephone	*Telephone*
Name	*Name*
Address	*Address*
Telephone	*Telephone*
Name	*Name*
Address	*Address*
Telephone	*Telephone*
Name	*Name*
Address	*Address*
Telephone	*Telephone*
Name	*Name*
Address	*Address*
Telephone	*Telephone*
Name	*Name*
Address	*Address*
Telephone	*Telephone*

Addresses

Name	*Name*
Address	*Address*
Telephone	*Telephone*
Name	*Name*
Address	*Address*
Telephone	*Telephone*
Name	*Name*
Address	*Address*
Telephone	*Telephone*
Name	*Name*
Address	*Address*
Telephone	*Telephone*
Name	*Name*
Address	*Address*
Telephone	*Telephone*
Name	*Name*
Address	*Address*
Telephone	*Telephone*
Name	*Name*
Address	*Address*
Telephone	*Telephone*
Name	*Name*
Address	*Address*
Telephone	*Telephone*

Addresses

Name	*Name*
Address	*Address*
Telephone	*Telephone*
Name	*Name*
Address	*Address*
Telephone	*Telephone*
Name	*Name*
Address	*Address*
Telephone	*Telephone*
Name	*Name*
Address	*Address*
Telephone	*Telephone*
Name	*Name*
Address	*Address*
Telephone	*Telephone*
Name	*Name*
Address	*Address*
Telephone	*Telephone*
Name	*Name*
Address	*Address*
Telephone	*Telephone*
Name	*Name*
Address	*Address*
Telephone	*Telephone*

Addresses

Name	*Name*
Address	*Address*
Telephone	*Telephone*
Name	*Name*
Address	*Address*
Telephone	*Telephone*
Name	*Name*
Address	*Address*
Telephone	*Telephone*
Name	*Name*
Address	*Address*
Telephone	*Telephone*
Name	*Name*
Address	*Address*
Telephone	*Telephone*
Name	*Name*
Address	*Address*
Telephone	*Telephone*
Name	*Name*
Address	*Address*
Telephone	*Telephone*
Name	*Name*
Address	*Address*
Telephone	*Telephone*

Notes

Notes

Fodor's Travel Guides

Available at bookstores everywhere, or call 1–800–533–6478, 24 hours a day.

U.S. Guides

Alaska

Arizona

Boston

California

Cape Cod, Martha's Vineyard, Nantucket

The Carolinas & the Georgia Coast

Chicago

Colorado

Florida

Hawaii

Las Vegas, Reno, Tahoe

Los Angeles

Maine, Vermont, New Hampshire

Maui

Miami & the Keys

New England

New Orleans

New York City

Pacific North Coast

Philadelphia & the Pennsylvania Dutch Country

The Rockies

San Diego

San Francisco

Santa Fe, Taos, Albuquerque

Seattle & Vancouver

The South

The U.S. & British Virgin Islands

The Upper Great Lakes Region

USA

Vacations in New York State

Vacations on the Jersey Shore

Virginia & Maryland

Waikiki

Walt Disney World and the Orlando Area

Washington, D.C.

Foreign Guides

Acapulco, Ixtapa, Zihuatanejo

Australia & New Zealand

Austria

The Bahamas

Baja & Mexico's Pacific Coast Resorts

Barbados

Berlin

Bermuda

Brazil

Brittany & Normandy

Budapest

Canada

Cancun, Cozumel, Yucatan Peninsula

Caribbean

China

Costa Rica, Belize, Guatemala

The Czech Republic & Slovakia

Eastern Europe

Egypt

Euro Disney

Europe

Europe's Great Cities

Florence & Tuscany

France

Germany

Great Britain

Greece

The Himalayan Countries

Hong Kong

India

Ireland

Israel

Italy

Japan

Kenya & Tanzania

Korea

London

Madrid & Barcelona

Mexico

Montreal & Quebec City

Morocco

Moscow & St. Petersburg

The Netherlands, Belgium & Luxembourg

New Zealand

Norway

Nova Scotia, Prince Edward Island & New Brunswick

Paris

Portugal

Provence & the Riviera

Rome

Russia & the Baltic Countries

Scandinavia

Scotland

Singapore

South America

Southeast Asia

Spain

Sweden

Switzerland

Thailand

Tokyo

Toronto

Turkey

Vienna & the Danube Valley

Yugoslavia

Special Series

Fodor's Affordables

Caribbean

Europe

Florida

France

Germany

Great Britain

London

Italy

Paris

Fodor's Bed & Breakfast and Country Inns Guides

Canada's Great Country Inns

California

Cottages, B&Bs and Country Inns of England and Wales

Mid-Atlantic Region

New England

The Pacific Northwest

The South

The Southwest

The Upper Great Lakes Region

The West Coast

The Berkeley Guides

California

Central America

Eastern Europe

France

Germany

Great Britain & Ireland

Mexico

Pacific Northwest & Alaska

San Francisco

Fodor's Exploring Guides

Australia

Britain

California

The Caribbean

Florida

France

Germany

Ireland

Italy

London

New York City

Paris

Rome

Singapore & Malaysia

Spain

Thailand

Fodor's Flashmaps

New York

Washington, D.C.

Fodor's Pocket Guides

Bahamas

Barbados

Jamaica

London

New York City

Paris

Puerto Rico

San Francisco

Washington, D.C.

Fodor's Sports

Cycling

Hiking

Running

Sailing

The Insider's Guide to the Best Canadian Skiing

Skiing in the USA & Canada

Fodor's Three-In-Ones (guidebook, language cassette, and phrase book)

France

Germany

Italy

Mexico

Spain

Fodor's Special-Interest Guides

Accessible USA

Cruises and Ports of Call

Euro Disney

Halliday's New England Food Explorer

Healthy Escapes

London Companion

Shadow Traffic's New York Shortcuts and Traffic Tips

Sunday in New York

Walt Disney World and the Orlando Area

Walt Disney World for Adults

Fodor's Touring Guides

Touring Europe

Touring USA: Eastern Edition

Fodor's Vacation Planners

Great American Vacations

National Parks of the East

National Parks of the West

The Wall Street Journal Guides to Business Travel

Europe

International Cities

Pacific Rim

USA & Canada

WHEREVER YOU TRAVEL, *H*ELP IS NEVER FAR AWAY.

From planning your trip to replacing
lost Cards, American Express® Travel Service
Offices* are always there to help.

BARBADOS

Barbados International Travel Service
McGregor Street
Bridgetown
809-431-2423